How Serious a Threat Is Climate Change?

Hal Marcovitz

INCONTROVERSY

ReferencePoint
Press®

San Diego, CA

© 2011 ReferencePoint Press, Inc.
Printed in the United States

For more information, contact:
ReferencePoint Press, Inc.
PO Box 27779
San Diego, CA 92198
www. ReferencePointPress.com

Picture Credits
AP Images: 7, 43
Mauricio Anton/Science Photo Library: 63
© Corbis/Arnd Wiegmann: 50
© Corbis/Bettmann: 13
© Corbis/Jon Bower/LOOP Images: 25
© Corbis/Pat O'Hara: 73
© Corbis/Peter Foley: 21
© Corbis/Pichi Chuang: 67
© Corbis/Wendy Stone: 60
iStockphoto.com: 40
Landov: 54
NASA, Goddard Institute for Space Studies/Science Photo Library: 31, 35

LIBRARY OF CONGRESS CATALOGING-IN-PUBLICATION DATA

Marcovitz, Hal.
  How serious a threat is climate change? / by Hal Marcovitz.
    p. cm. — (In controversy)
  Includes bibliographical references and index.
  ISBN-13: 978-1-60152-142-2 (hardcover)
  ISBN-10: 1-60152-142-1 (hardcover)
  1. Environmental management. 2. Environmental protection. 3. Global warming.
  4. Environmentalism. I. Title.
  TD170.15.M37 2011
  363.738'74—dc22
                                                              2010033916

Contents

Foreword   4

Introduction
  The Vanishing Village   6

Chapter One
  What Are the Origins of the Climate
  Change Controversy?   10

Chapter Two
  How Reliable Is the Science of Climate Change?   24

Chapter Three
  What Are the Potential Economic Impacts of
  Climate Change?   39

Chapter Four
  What Are the Potential Environmental Impacts
  of Climate Change?   53

Chapter Five
  How Has the World Responded to Climate Change?   66

Related Organizations and Web Sites   79
Additional Reading   83
Source Notes   85
Index   92
About the Author   96

Foreword

In 2008, as the U.S. economy and economies worldwide were falling into the worst recession since the Great Depression, most Americans had difficulty comprehending the complexity, magnitude, and scope of what was happening. As is often the case with a complex, controversial issue such as this historic global economic recession, looking at the problem as a whole can be overwhelming and often does not lead to understanding. One way to better comprehend such a large issue or event is to break it into smaller parts. The intricacies of global economic recession may be difficult to understand, but one can gain insight by instead beginning with an individual contributing factor such as the real estate market. When examined through a narrower lens, complex issues become clearer and easier to evaluate.

This is the idea behind ReferencePoint Press's *In Controversy* series. The series examines the complex, controversial issues of the day by breaking them into smaller pieces. Rather than looking at the stem cell research debate as a whole, a title would examine an important aspect of the debate such as *Is Stem Cell Research Necessary?* or *Is Embryonic Stem Cell Research Ethical?* By studying the central issues of the debate individually, researchers gain a more solid and focused understanding of the topic as a whole.

Each book in the series provides a clear, insightful discussion of the issues, integrating facts and a variety of contrasting opinions for a solid, balanced perspective. Personal accounts and direct quotes from academic and professional experts, advocacy groups, politicians, and others enhance the narrative. Sidebars add depth to the discussion by expanding on important ideas and events. For quick reference, a list of key facts concludes every chapter. Source notes, an annotated organizations list, bibliography, and index provide student researchers with additional tools for papers and class discussion.

The *In Controversy* series also challenges students to think critically about issues, to improve their problem-solving skills, and to sharpen their ability to form educated opinions. As President Barack Obama stated in a March 2009 speech, success in the twenty-first century will not be measurable merely by students' ability to "fill in a bubble on a test but whether they possess 21st century skills like problem-solving and critical thinking and entrepreneurship and creativity." Those who possess these skills will have a strong foundation for whatever lies ahead.

No one can know for certain what sort of world awaits today's students. What we can assume, however, is that those who are inquisitive about a wide range of issues; open-minded to divergent views; aware of bias and opinion; and able to reason, reflect, and reconsider will be best prepared for the future. As the international development organization Oxfam notes, "Today's young people will grow up to be the citizens of the future: but what that future holds for them is uncertain. We can be quite confident, however, that they will be faced with decisions about a wide range of issues on which people have differing, contradictory views. If they are to develop as global citizens all young people should have the opportunity to engage with these controversial issues."

In Controversy helps today's students better prepare for tomorrow. An understanding of the complex issues that drive our world and the ability to think critically about them are essential components of contributing, competing, and succeeding in the twenty-first century.

The Vanishing Village

Sarichef is a small island that is part of Alaska, located just below the Arctic Circle. It is no more than a quarter-mile (0.4km) across and two miles (3.2km) long. Despite the long winters and harsh living conditions, Sarichef has been occupied for centuries by Eskimo people known as the Inupiat. The lone village on the island is Shishmaref, where the population hovers around 600.

About two decades ago, the people of Shishmaref started noticing a change on the island—the spring thaw seemed to be starting earlier, while the winters appeared to be milder and starting later. While those conditions may sound as though they would be a pleasant change for the Inupiat, that has not been the case. The Inupiat rely on the hard ice pack to drive their snowmobiles 20 miles (32.2km) or more off the island and across the frozen ocean surface to track game including seals, walruses, moose, rabbits, and migratory birds. Now, as the spring hunting season commences, the surface grows mushy, meaning their snowmobiles fail to gain traction on the ice. As a result, the Inupiat find themselves hunting closer to home and bagging less game.

Other changes have also occurred on Sarichef. The longer springs and autumns have brought more severe storms. In 1997 a huge late autumn storm washed away the northern edge of Shishmaref, destroying several homes. In 2001 more homes were damaged when storms blew 12-foot waves (3.6m) across the island. Finally, the residents of Shishmaref realized they had no choice: They voted to abandon their homes and leave the island. "The land is going away," said

"The land is going away. I think it's going to vanish one of these days."[1]

—Shelton Kokeok, 65, who has lived on the island of Sarichef his whole life.

Shelton Kokeok, 65, who has lived in Shishmaref his whole life. "I think it's going to vanish one of these days."[1]

The Canary in the Coal Mine

For many scientists, political leaders, and environmentalists, the conditions in Shishmaref provide ample evidence that climate change is a scientific fact and represents a genuine threat to the future of civilization on earth. According to scientists, climate change is caused by carbon dioxide and other so-called "greenhouse gases" that are emitted through the burning of fossil fuels, such as coal and oil. Just as panes of glass in a greenhouse roof trap sunlight, these gases remain in the atmosphere, trap the heat from the sun, and cause the earth to warm.

Already, they argue, global warming has affected not only places like Shishmaref but other corners of the planet as well. For example, the forests of Canada are slowly receding because wood-destroying pests, such as pine bark beetles, are thriving due to the warmer and shorter winters. Along the New England coast, the lobster harvest is smaller than in years past because lobsters thrive in chilly waters, but since the ocean temperature has been rising, populations of lobsters are declining. Across America, scientists

An abandoned house in the Alaskan Inupiat village of Shishmaref slides into the sea. Mild winters and early spring thaws have raised sea levels and eroded significant portions of the village, forcing residents to abandon their homes.

have noticed fewer varieties of wildflowers and more wild grasses that grow in warmer temperatures. Meanwhile, people have to endure larger swarms of mosquitoes, which increase when summers are longer and hotter. In tropical climates, the warmer conditions have spawned larger populations of disease-carrying insects, such as mosquitoes that spread malaria.

But nowhere else on earth, they argue, has global warming more directly affected people's lives than it has in Shishmaref. Says Gunter Weller, director of the University of Alaska's Center for Global Change, "Shishmaref is an indication of what to expect in the future in other parts of the world. In that respect it is the canary in the coal mine."[2]

Disputing the Evidence

Despite mounting evidence of a warming climate, many scientists, political leaders, and others remain skeptical. They contend that changes in earth's climate are natural and not caused by fossil fuel emissions. Moreover, many refuse to accept the scientific evidence of climate change and instead cite other scientific data that support their positions. Says Edmund Contoski, an author and former urban planner who is an avowed skeptic of the greenhouse gas effect, "The global warming advocates make all sorts of false claims about dire consequences of global warming. They claim it will result in the spread of malaria, food shortages, more human deaths, more violent weather, and a loss of biological diversity through the extinction of species. All untrue."[3]

Indeed, Contoski and other skeptics insist that the very coldest places on earth—places like Shishmaref—are not warming at all. Peter C. Glover, editor of a European energy journal, points to evidence showing that temperatures in the Antarctic are at their lowest point in the past 50 years and that the surface of Antarctic ice has actually grown in recent years. "The fact is . . . the world's ice mass has been expanding not contracting, which will surprise evening news junkies fed a diet of polar bears floating about on ice floes and snow shelves falling into the oceans," he says. "The

"The world's ice mass has been expanding not contracting, which will surprise evening news junkies fed a diet of polar bears floating about on ice floes and snow shelves falling into the oceans."[4]

—Peter C. Glover, editor of a European energy journal.

fact that the world's ice mass is expanding not contracting is plainly of seismic importance in the climate debate."[4]

A Question of Survival

Whether the ice around Sarichef is melting because of a natural warming cycle or because of greenhouse gas emissions, the people of Shishmaref know their time in the village is limited. Morris Kiyutelluk and his family have already been forced to move. During a recent storm, the Kiyutelluks heard waves slapping against the outside of their home. The force of the waves was so strong that the floors and walls started shaking. Fearing for their lives, the Kiyutelluks fled their home. After the storm, the family moved to the other side of the island; eventually, the Kiyutelluks expect to leave Sarichef. Taking a visitor to the site of his former home, Kiyutelluk pointed to what is now a shallow pool of slushy water. He said, "That's where I grew up."[5]

As the people of Shishmaref prepare to leave their homes, the debate over climate change will continue. On one side stand scientists, politicians, and others who are convinced that fossil fuel emissions must be curbed or else people across the globe will face the same fate as the Inupiat—meaning they will be uprooted and forced to abandon ways of life they have known for decades if not centuries. On the other side stand scientists and politicians who are just as steadfast in their beliefs that over the course of history, earth has gone through a number of warming and cooling cycles, and civilization has always found a way to survive.

Facts

- A 2009 report by the U.S. Government Accountability Office identified 31 Alaskan villages threatened by coastal erosion or flooding caused by climate change.
- Measurements have indicated that ocean water has been swallowing up the island of Sarichef at a rate of about 10 feet (3m) per year.

What Are the Origins of the Climate Change Controversy?

Many people became believers in global warming on June 23, 1988. That day found Americans sweltering in some of the hottest temperatures on record—the thermometer reached 100°F (37.8°C) or more in some 45 U.S. cities. It seemed as though no part of the country was spared from the heat wave—in Sacramento, California, the thermometer hit 102°F (38.9°C) while in Lincoln, Nebraska, the temperature reached 103°F (39.4°C). On the East Coast, people in Richmond, Virginia, saw their thermometers reach 101°F (38.3°C). According to meteorologists, the first five months of 1988 were warmer than any comparable period on record since scientists started charting temperature trends in 1852.

Certainly, Americans had experienced hot weather before, but this time the high temperatures were punctuated with a warning issued from a U.S. Senate hearing room in Washington, D.C. On June 23, 1988, as the temperatures soared outside, National Aeronautics and Space Administration (NASA) climate scientist James E. Hansen told senators why it was so hot. "The greenhouse effect," he said, "has been detected and is changing our climate right now." Hansen said that he arrived at his conclusion with "99 percent confidence."[6]

At that time, few people outside the scientific community had heard of the greenhouse effect or the theory of climate change. Most people were more concerned with the price and availability of gasoline than with the notion that simply by driving to work or school in the morning they were helping bring about the demise of the planet. In fact, Hansen's remarks before the Senate were met with a healthy dose of skepticism. "Climate may indeed change, with or without human interference," insisted S. Fred Singer, a professor of environmental science at the University of Virginia, "but there won't be palm trees in New York, cotton in Toronto or wheat in Labrador—even by the year 2100."[7]

Heat-Trapping Gases

Although members of the Senate may have been hearing about the greenhouse effect for the first time on that summer day in 1988, scientists had been looking at how different gases affect earth's temperature at least since 1824. In that year French mathematician Jean Baptiste Joseph Fourier suggested that some gases let in sunlight but then trap the sun's radiation, warming the earth.

Fourier was not looking specifically at how fossil fuel use affected the atmosphere. At the time, the coal-fired steam engine was still in its infancy, while widespread use of the gasoline-powered internal combustion engine was still decades in the future. Instead, Fourier's calculations showed that without an atmosphere to trap heat, earth would be a much colder place. Fourier compared the atmosphere to a glass vessel.

In 1859 British physicist James Tyndall tested a number of gases to see which trapped the most solar radiation. He concluded that oxygen and nitrogen, which compose 99 percent of earth's atmosphere, have no heat-trapping properties at all. However, his experiments found that a number of other gases do trap solar radiation—among those gases are carbon dioxide.

Power for the Industrial Age

By the end of the nineteenth century, oil, coal, and natural gas—all of which emit carbon dioxide when they burn—emerged as primary sources of fuel, powering the Industrial Age that had

> "The greenhouse effect has been detected and is changing our climate right now."[6]
>
> — National Aeronautics and Space Administration climate scientist James E. Hansen.

What Is Mean Temperature Change?

According to the National Aeronautics and Space Administration (NASA), the mean temperature of earth has increased about 1.5°F (0.9°C) in the 100 years between 1910 and 2010. Certainly, most people would hardly notice such a slight difference, but many scientists still regard the temperature change as significant.

The change represents the mean difference in temperature, which refers to the average change in temperatures everywhere on earth throughout the year. Therefore, while the temperature change probably will not be noticed in a place like New Mexico, where the average temperature has risen just 1°F (0.6°C) in the past 100 years, the average difference in Alaska has been much greater.

According to the University of Alaska Climate Research Center, the average temperature in Alaska has risen by 3°F (1.8°C) just since 1949. And in Barrow, Alaska, one of the northernmost places in the state, the average temperature has risen by nearly 5°F (2.8°C) since 1949. Says a NASA report, "In reality, the temperature change has not been consistent across the planet. . . . The increase in temperature has not been consistent through time, either. Some periods during the year have experienced greater and faster temperature increases than others."

National Aeronautics and Space Administration, "Remote Sensing: Temperature," November 10, 2004. www.cotf.edu.

swept through Europe and America. By then, coal had long been in use as a fuel for homes, ships, locomotives, schools, industrial plants, office buildings, and other facilities.

Meanwhile, the energy-producing qualities of oil had been discovered. During the first half of the nineteenth century, most lamps were fueled with oil distilled from whale fat, which is known as blubber. This type of oil was very expensive—whales had to be hunted down by ships that often ventured thousands of miles from their home ports. The whales had to be harpooned, dragged on board, and slaughtered. The voyages usually took months. Could oil be found cheaper and closer to home? Entrepreneurs knew that for years Native Americans had used oil, skimmed off the surfaces of lakes, to make their canoes waterproof as well as for ingredients in medicine. The oil could be found underground, where it would occasionally seep up to the surface through cracks in the earth.

On August 27, 1859, Edwin Drake, a former railroad conductor, sank the first oil well near Titusville, Pennsylvania. Oil oozed to the surface, where it was stored in wooden barrels. Although his methods were crude, and his workers drilled just 70 feet (21.3m) down, Drake's well was virtually the same as the wells that are today drilled thousands of feet below earth's surface by the world's biggest oil companies.

Edwin Drake sank the world's first commercial oil well in 1859, launching an oil boom in western Pennsylvania (pictured). Since that time, oil has reigned as one of humanity's most important fuels.

Dependence on Oil

In the ensuing decades oil would grow into an important fuel for many industrial purposes as well as for a new generation of ships. By the early years of the twentieth century, a number of energy sources were being employed to power the world's first automobiles, among them the electric motor, steam engine, and gasoline-burning internal combustion engine.

Indeed, inventors had been tinkering with the internal combustion engine since the 1820s, and by the 1860s they were using it to power some of the first automobiles, which were built largely from bicycle parts and similar crude components. Electric motors had their drawbacks—batteries could power cars only briefly before they lost their charges. Steam engines were more powerful—but they were heavy, unreliable, and often hard to start. And even though the engines employed steam under pressure to power the automobile, they were not divorced entirely from oil: The steam was heated by burners that were fueled by gasoline or kerosene.

In 1908 carmaker Henry Ford decided to employ an internal combustion engine to power his Model T, the world's first mass-produced car. "The automobile . . . could not be successfully developed until the internal combustion engine had been invented," Ford said later. "Earlier engines, such as steam engines, were too heavy; they weighed too much per horsepower to be practical for use . . . but with the coming of the internal combustion engine it was possible to concentrate in a small place a small weight and an enormous amount of power. Thus, it enabled us to develop the automobile."[8]

Between 1908 and 1927 Ford Motor Company sold 15 million Model Ts. By then, of course, Ford's competitors were also mass-producing automobiles as well as trucks, and virtually all of them were powered by gasoline or diesel fuel, which is also a refined form of oil. The development of the internal combustion engine may have helped establish the automotive industry in America and Europe, but it also meant cars would be completely dependent on oil, sparking a massive search for oil reserves that eventually reached across the globe. The aviation industry, which

> "Climate may indeed change, with or without human interference, but there won't be palm trees in New York, cotton in Toronto or wheat in Labrador—even by the year 2100."[7]
>
> — S. Fred Singer, professor of environmental science at the University of Virginia.

would explode in the twentieth century, is also completely dependent on oil-based fuels.

Concern About the Atmosphere

As Ford and other entrepreneurs were revolutionizing transportation and making breakthroughs in other areas of industry, scientists were starting to study the impact of these developments on the atmosphere. Indeed, in 1896—12 years before the first Model T rolled out of Ford's factory—Swedish physicist Svante Arrhenius published a paper titled *On the Influence of Carbonic Acid in the Air upon the Temperature on the Ground*. In the paper, Arrhenius suggested that carbon dioxide and other gases in the atmosphere trap heat, which is absorbed by the oceans and terrain of the planet.

In 1937 University of Wisconsin geography professor Glen Thomas Trewartha coined the term "greenhouse effect" when he explained in the college textbook *An Introduction to Weather and Climate* that the atmosphere is "like a pane of glass in a greenhouse . . . thus maintaining surface temperatures considerably higher than they otherwise would be."[9] And in 1951 Guy Stewart Callendar of Great Britain published a paper asserting that the carbon dioxide content of earth's atmosphere had increased by 10 percent since the 1890s. Callendar was not a scientist—he was an engineer who specialized in steam power. Nevertheless, his findings prompted others with expertise in chemistry, meteorology, and similar sciences to begin taking a hard look at the issue of climate change.

The Keeling Curve

One of those scientists was Charles Keeling, who developed instruments that could detect carbon dioxide in the atmosphere down to one part per million, meaning that his instruments could tell whether a sample of air was composed of as little as 1/1,000,000 of carbon dioxide. Keeling started taking readings in 1958. He placed his device at the top of Mauna Loa, a 13,000-foot-high volcano (3,962m) on the big island of Hawaii—certainly, one of the most pristine places on earth, far from the pollution one finds in cities.

Svante Arrhenius

Swedish physicist Svante Arrhenius is regarded as one of the pioneers in climate change research. His 1896 paper *On the Influence of Carbonic Acid in the Air upon the Temperature on the Ground* found that very slight changes in the carbon dioxide content of the atmosphere could result in dramatic effects on the environment of earth. He predicted that a tripling of the amount of carbon in the air could result in a rise in Arctic temperatures of 16°F (9°C).

However, Arrhenius was not convinced that the warming of the planet's surface was anything to be terribly concerned about. In contrast, Arrhenius predicted that a warming of earth's surface would enhance plant growth and help farmers grow crops. He predicted that worldwide hunger could be less of a problem in a warmer world. As for people who live in very cold places, Arrhenius suggested they would learn to appreciate the warmer weather. "We may hope to enjoy ages with more equable and better climates, especially as regards the colder regions of the Earth," he said.

Quoted in David Malakoff, "Revisiting the 'Keeling Curve,'" National Public Radio, January 28, 2009. www.npr.org.

Keeling died in 2005, but others have continued taking readings from the Mauna Loa station as well as other places on earth. Many scientists believe those readings reflect an alarming trend. The results, which are known as the Keeling Curve, show a definite upsurge in the amount of carbon dioxide found in the atmosphere. In 1958 Keeling's readings showed 315 parts per million (ppm) of carbon dioxide in earth's atmosphere. By 1990 readings showed 355 ppm; in 2005, 379 ppm; and in 2010 the readings recorded carbon content of 389 ppm. In other words, in just 50 years of testing, the carbon content of the atmosphere had grown by nearly 25 percent. "It was the discovery of the *possibility* of global warming," physicist and science historian Spencer R. Weart says of Keeling's work. "Experts would continue for many years to argue over what would actually happen to the planet's climate. But no longer could a well-informed scientist dismiss out of hand the possibility that our emission of greenhouse gases would warm the Earth."[10]

Although Keeling's work concentrated on measuring the carbon content of the atmosphere, other gases used in consumer and industrial applications were also found to be contributing to the greenhouse effect. According to the U.S. Energy Department, carbon dioxide makes up 84 percent of the greenhouse gas content of the atmosphere. Another greenhouse gas is methane, which makes up 9 percent. Methane is emitted from landfills and wastewater treatment; it is also a byproduct of incineration as well as oil and coal use.

Nitrous oxide, which makes up 5 percent of the atmosphere's greenhouse gas content, is emitted from animal manure and wastewater treatment and is also a byproduct of incineration and fossil fuel use. (Surgeons and dentists also use nitrous oxide as an anesthetic—it is commonly known as "laughing gas.") The final 2 percent of greenhouse gas content is composed of chemicals known as hydrofluorocarbons, perfluorocarbons, and sulfur hexafluoride. These gases are used in assorted industrial and consumer-based applications, such as aerosol cans.

A Climate Crisis

As Keeling gathered and released his statistics on carbon content, many scientific organizations reviewed his results as well as studies performed by other atmospheric specialists. These organizations started putting the weight of their influence behind the studies, arguing that alternatives to fossil fuels had to be found in order to halt global warming. In 1979 the National Academy of Sciences issued a report confirming that global warming is a consequence of fossil fuel use and stating that a doubling of carbon content of the atmosphere—at the time about 340 ppm, according to the Keeling Curve—would cause the average temperature of the planet to rise as much as 8.1°F (4.5°C).

> "Experts would continue for many years to argue over what would actually happen to the planet's climate. But no longer could a well-informed scientist dismiss out of hand the possibility that our emission of greenhouse gases would warm the Earth."[10]
>
> — Physicist and science historian Spencer R. Weart.

Many environmental groups embraced the cause and started advocating for development of renewable energy—solar and wind among other sources—to replace oil and coal. They also called on Congress and leaders of other governments to pass laws capping carbon emissions. Among the most influential of the environmentalists is former vice president Al Gore who, after leaving office in 2001, became an advocate for clean energy. Gore's books and films have helped raise awareness of a problem that was unknown by most people just two decades before when Hansen testified before the U.S. Senate. Gore's work has been recognized with a Nobel Peace Prize. "Now comes the threat of climate crisis—a threat that is real, rising, imminent, and universal," Gore said in his 2007 Nobel acceptance speech. "Once again, it is the 11th hour. The penalties for ignoring this challenge are immense and growing, and at some near point would be unsustainable and unrecoverable."[11]

Skeptics Emerge

While Gore and many scientists warned of grave consequences ahead, some critics questioned their predictions. Indeed, soon after Hansen completed his testimony before the Senate panel, skeptics stepped forward questioning the scientific data offered as evidence that human activity, through the burning of fossil fuels, is responsible for global warming.

Singer pointed out that over the course of millions of years, earth has warmed and cooled in natural cycles. Singer said he did not doubt that more greenhouse gases had been expelled into the atmosphere than ever before. However, he insisted that if the planet is going through a warming trend or cooling trend, it would not matter how much carbon dioxide is in the atmosphere, the temperature of earth would change.

Moreover, Singer cited statistics showing that since the late nineteenth century, when fossil fuel use greatly expanded, scientific data indicated that some warming had occurred but the trend was inconsistent. Singer cited statistics showing that from 1880 to 1940 the temperature of the planet increased by 1°F (0.6°C), while from 1940 to 1965 the temperature dropped a bit, followed by a sudden surge of about 0.3°F (0.2°C). "Congress has heard from a reputable scientist, James E. Hansen . . . who is '99 percent sure' that the greenhouse effect 'is here,'" said Singer. "Other reputable but less vocal atmospheric scientists estimate the rise as much less, however."[12]

To other skeptics, a planet-wide average temperature rise of just 8°F (4.8°C) over the course of what is sure to be several decades did not seem terribly threatening. Bjørn Lomborg, a Danish author and statistician, wondered whether anybody would notice such a slight increase in the average temperature. Moreover, Lomborg and others suggest cutting back fossil fuel use would have a devastating effect on the world economy—shutting factories, closing down transportation routes, and making oil unavailable for its use in plastics and chemicals. He says, "Global warming, though its size and future projections are both unrealistically pessimistic, is almost certainly taking place, but the typical cure of early and radical fossil fuel cutbacks is way worse than the original affliction, and moreover its total impact will not pose a devastating problem for our future."[13]

"From the scientific point of view, in terms of large scale climate cycles, we are in a period of cooling."[17]

— Russian climate expert Arkady Tishkov.

Doubts About Global Warming

And some skeptics even wondered whether earth is warming at all. Just months before Hansen testified before Congress, some areas of Europe experienced their coldest winters in decades. In January 1987 a record low temperature of -49°F (-45°C) was recorded in Norway's Kjørlen Mountains. In the French skiing town of Bessans, a record low temperature of -24°F (-31°C) was set. Even in places in France where it is not supposed to get very cold, citizens shivered through a blustery winter. In Marseille, a French city located on the otherwise warm and sunny shores of the Mediterranean Sea, citizens saw their first snowfall in decades. Russia was also experiencing one of the country's coldest winters on record. "You'd be hard pressed to convince the [Russians] that the Earth is getting warmer,"[14] said meteorologist Gail Martell.

Indeed, months after Hansen testified at the Senate hearing, meteorologists announced that the soaring temperatures of 1988 had nothing to do with climate change. They were instead caused by a mass of tropical ocean current and air pressure in the Pacific Ocean that forced the North American continent to endure high heat. This mass of water currents and air pressure is known as El Niño—Spanish for "the boy," a reference to the Christ child because weather patterns associated with El Niño often begin around Christmastime. Every three to six years the water and air currents of El Niño circulate across great swaths of the Pacific Ocean, creating atmospheric changes that affect the weather—often making it extremely hot or sometimes unseasonably cool. After concluding that El Niño had been responsible for the 1988 heat wave, meteorologists said they expected the weather in the near future to set no temperature records. "We're looking for next summer and fall to be more or less normal,"[15] said Tim Barnett of the Scripps Institute of Oceanography in La Jolla, California, in January 1989.

Frigid Winter, Sweltering Summer

Since Europe's winter of 1987–1988 and North America's summer of 1988, other wild swings in the weather have occurred. In the winter of 2009–2010, northern Europe again experienced one of its coldest winters on record. In Siberia, an area of Russia near the Arctic Circle, meteorologists said it was quite possibly the coldest winter on record. During the cold snap, temperatures recorded on 63 days dropped to lows of -13°F (-25°C). "When we say that this winter in Siberia was record breaking, we are aware that temperatures on some days of other years may have gone lower, but in the most recent winter the substantial cold was staying longer than usual and over larger regions than usual,"[16] said Dmitry Kiktev, deputy head of the Russian meteorological service Rosgidromet.

More than just Siberia was affected by the cold blast—in other parts of Russia, wintry temperatures persisted into mid-April 2010. "Of course we can't say that global warming is a myth and falsification. In many regions of the planet the temperature is higher than expected because of human impact," said Russian climate expert Arkady Tishkov. "But the climate system of the planet is changing according to different cycles. . . . From the scientific point of view, in terms of large scale climate cycles, we are in a period of cooling."[17]

On the other side of the globe, people hardly considered themselves living in a period of cooling temperatures. During the summer of 2010 Americans in many cities sweltered in record-breaking heat. Eventually, climate scientists at NASA declared the summer of 2010 the hottest on record. In New York City, for example, the temperature hit 103 degrees on July 7. Similar record-breaking temperatures were set in such cities as Boston, Philadelphia, and Providence, Rhode Island. As in 1988, though, the true culprit was not global warming but another visit from El Niño.

Weather Versus Climate

Conservative pundits soon weighed in, arguing that the recent colder-than-average winters disproved the science supporting global warming. In February 2010, as many East Coast cities dug out of a huge regional snowfall, representatives from the right-wing media celebrated what they were sure was a victory against people they characterized as climate change alarmists. An editorial in the conservative *Washington Times* huffed, "Those who value freedom should thank Mother Nature for her sense of humor, undermining the case for global warming one flake at a time. So

Seeking relief from record-breaking heat, a young New Yorker sticks his head in a sprinkler during the summer of 2010. Scientists say an El Niño weather system resulted in extreme cold in Siberia and unusually high temperatures in New York City in 2010.

although we're quite tired of shoveling, we say, 'Bring on the blizzard.'"[18] Added Fox News Channel host Steve Doocy, "It's interesting, though, given the fact that the weather is so rotten right now that people are going, 'How can there be global warming if it's snowing and it's fairly cold?'"[19]

In response, experts who support the science of global warming insist that discussion about climate change must be separated from talk about the weather and that an occasional cool summer or frigid winter should give no one pause to question global warming. They acknowledge that periodic weather patterns like El Niño have a lot to do with affecting the day-to-day weather in a region of the planet. But overall, they say, earth is warming, and eventually, climate change will cause all manner of environmental chaos. "The difference between weather and climate is a measure of time," says Rob Gutro of NASA.

> Weather is what conditions of the atmosphere are over a short period of time, and climate is how the atmosphere "behaves" over relatively long periods of time. . . . In most places, weather can change from minute-to-minute, hour-to-hour, day-to-day, and season-to-season. Climate, however, is the average of weather over time and space. An easy way to remember the difference is that climate is what you expect, like a very hot summer, and weather is what you get, like a hot day with pop-up thunderstorms.[20]

During the past two centuries, many scientists, political leaders, and environmental activists have accepted the evidence that fossil fuel use is a factor in climate change. Others question the science, pointing out that the evidence of the greenhouse effect is not yet conclusive. And while scientists will continue following the Keeling Curve and other methods for charting climate change, the discussion has now moved into the political arena, the media, and other public forums, suggesting that its resolution will not be decided atop remote volcanoes in Hawaii or in Siberian wastelands but in places like Washington, D.C., and other world capitals, where the debate is sure to remain as hot as the weather.

Facts

- The World Meteorological Society declared the 2000 decade the warmest decade on record dating back to the mid-nineteenth century, when the organization first started compiling data.

- In 1997 the Vostok station in Antarctica, a scientific outpost maintained by the Russian government, recorded a temperature of -132°F (-91°C). It is believed to be the lowest temperature ever recorded anywhere on earth.

- Scientists have calculated that in the thirteenth century, the carbon dioxide content of the atmosphere was 280 parts per million. Nearly seven centuries later, Charles Keeling's first readings showed the carbon content of the atmosphere had increased by about 11 percent.

- When National Aeronautics and Space Administration climate scientist James E. Hansen testified before the U.S. Senate in 1988, he predicted that the average temperature of earth could rise by as much as 9°F (5°C) by 2050.

- The fossil fuels—oil, coal, and natural gas—have been buried beneath the surface of earth since a geological era known as the Carboniferous Period, which occurred from 286 million to 360 million years ago.

- A barrel of oil contains about 44 gallons (166.6L). A single barrel produces about 19.5 gallons (72L) of gasoline, 9.2 gallons (35L) of home heating oil, and 4.1 gallons (15.5L) of jet fuel. The rest is devoted to various other uses, including lubricants, kerosene, and oil used to repair and repave roads.

How Reliable Is the Science of Climate Change?

In the years since Charles Keeling set up his instruments atop Mauna Loa, other scientists have fanned out across the globe to conduct their own experiments. They have performed numerous tests, and many have confirmed evidence of climate change. For example, in Asia scientists have trekked high into the Himalayas where they have conducted tests across the vast Tibetan Plateau, a 40,000-square-mile region (103,600 sq km) that contains the world's largest collection of ice outside the polar regions. Since the 1960s, scientists have studied the glaciers in the plateau, and have concluded that they are melting. Indeed, a 2007 study found that one-fifth of the ice in the Tibetan Plateau has disappeared since 1960. "The warming of the past 20 years is getting more and more intense," says Yao Tandong, head of China's Institute of Tibetan Plateau Research. "If warming continues, [the impact] will be even more serious."[21]

The governments of China, Bhutan, Nepal, Pakistan, and India are watching the outcome of the Tibetan Plateau research very closely, because rivers that originate in the plateau flow into those countries. One of the consequences of global warming is believed to be rising water levels—due to melting glaciers and polar ice caps as well as an increase in rainfall. (A warmer atmosphere tends to hold moisture longer, which means in a warmer world, it would rain more.) One study, published in the journal *Science*, predicted that the world's sea level would rise by some 20 feet (6m) by the end of the twenty-first century.

Therefore, the millions of people who live in close proximity to rivers that originate in the Tibetan Plateau could find themselves victims of flash floods that would occur as the waters rise and storms sweep through their communities. That effect would only be temporary, though. Eventually, as the glaciers melt, the rivers fed by the ice in the Tibetan Plateau would dry up, leaving millions without water. "This isn't like the polar ice caps," says Shubash Lohani, a Nepalese official of the World Wildlife Fund. "You have a huge population downstream from the Himalayas who are dependent on [the plateau]."[22]

Climate Changes over Time

The Tibetan Plateau data are accumulated much the same way that the Mauna Loa carbon readings are gauged: Scientists set

Snowmelt feeds one of the many lakes found on the Tibetan Plateau in the Himalayas. Surrounded by the planet's tallest mountains, earth's highest and largest plateau contains the largest collection of ice outside of the polar regions. Scientists say the glaciers there are melting, a result of a warming climate.

up instruments and periodically check them to learn results. In the Tibetan Plateau, scientists have driven stakes, equipped with global positioning devices, into the glaciers. These stakes provide baseline data on the sizes and locations of the glaciers. To learn the degree to which the glaciers are shrinking, the Tibetan Plateau researchers rely on satellite images provided by NASA. Meanwhile, instruments are employed to gauge the amount of carbon in the air in the vicinity of the glaciers. "Putting all this together, we can begin to get a reasonable estimate of the regional melt,"[23] says NASA atmospheric scientist Eric Wilcox.

While these types of experiments rely on proven scientific techniques as well as such high-tech instrumentation as satellites and global positioning devices, a large group of scientists has found many reasons to question the research. They claim that it fails to show the true picture of earth's climate situation.

The most significant argument made by these scientists is that most of the data show how earth's climate is purported to have changed over a matter of a few years or decades—a tiny fraction in the life of the planet. To learn the true nature of how earth's climate evolves, they argue, scientists must study the changes as they have occurred over hundreds of millions of years. "We geologists have always recognized that climate changes over time," says Australian geologist and global warming skeptic Ian Plimer. "Where we differ from a lot of people . . . is in our understanding of scale. They're only interested in the last 150 years. Our time frame is 4.5 billion years."[24]

Plimer says geological evidence shows that polar ice has often melted and reformed over the history of the planet and that carbon dioxide makes up a tiny fraction of the atmosphere. This essentially means that the earth's climate has changed many times over the life of the planet, independent of the content of fossil fuel emissions.

> "We geologists have always recognized that climate changes over time. Where we differ from a lot of people . . . is in our understanding of scale. They're only interested in the last 150 years. Our time frame is 4.5 billion years."[24]
>
> — Ian Plimer, Australian geologist.

The Hockey Stick Graph

In many fields, historical data (and numbers in general) can be used to both prove—and disprove—the same basic point. This is also the case with the science of climate change. In 1998

The Climate Confidence Crisis

While scientists spar over the soundness of the science that supports the greenhouse effect, a growing portion of the public believes the dangers of global warming are exaggerated. A poll taken by the Gallup Organization in 2010 found that 48 percent of Americans believe the threat of global warming is exaggerated. In 2009, 41 percent of Americans held that belief, and in 1997 a total of 31 percent of Americans believed the threat of climate change is exaggerated.

Some leaders of the scientific community admit they have done a poor job in public outreach. Scientists have often taken the attitude that their research should speak for itself. Meanwhile, oil companies and other industry groups sponsor TV advertising, Internet pages, and other forms of communication to get their messages across.

Climate scientist Judith Curry of the Georgia Institute of Technology feels that climate experts should be doing more to make their cases on the Internet. "Additional scientific voices entering the public debate particularly in the blogosphere would help in the broader communication efforts and in rebuilding trust," she says. "The openness and democratization of knowledge enabled by the Internet can be a tremendous tool for building public understanding of climate science and also trust in climate research."

Quoted in Andrew Freeman, "How to Calm the Climate Science Confidence Crisis," *Washington Post*, March 9, 2010. http://voices.washingtonpost.com.

climate scientists Ray Bradley of the University of Massachusetts, Malcolm Hughes of the University of Arizona, and Michael Mann of Pennsylvania State University collaborated on a scientific study that they believe strongly supports the theory of climate change.

The study presents a graph, which the scientists call the hockey stick graph. It shows how, over the past 1,000 years, the climate of earth remained relatively stable. In 1900, as the Industrial Age dominated life on the planet, earth's temperature suddenly started rising at a steep angle—evidence, they suggest, that the emissions of greenhouse gases have influenced earth's climate.

The handle of the hockey stick represents the years of stability, while the blade represents the sudden upsurge. To construct the graph, the scientists gathered data on how some tree trunks featured fewer rings, the deterioration of coral reefs, and the temperatures and compositions of ice found in the polar regions.

Environmentalists believe the hockey stick graph is one of the most important pieces of evidence to have emerged in years, supporting the notion that earth is warming. Says Gore, "The hockey stick graph . . . is proving to be completely true. Basically the graph shows the temperatures remain consistent for 1,000 years, and then, when the industrial revolution took place, temperatures spiked."[25]

In 2001 the United Nations Intergovernmental Panel on Climate Change (IPCC) published what is regarded as one of the bedrock studies in support of the science of global warming. In the study, the IPCC included the hockey stick graph to help support its contention that climate change is caused by fossil fuel emissions. For its work in providing scientific evidence behind the theory of climate change, the IPCC was awarded the Nobel Prize, which the panel shared with Gore.

Missing Facts

However, the hockey stick graph soon fell under scrutiny by skeptics, who questioned its accuracy. Critics of the graph charged that Mann, Hughes, and Bradley had left out key data—some of which was readily available through published records of weather patterns. One critic, University of Delaware climatologist David R. Legates, said the hockey stick graph did not employ evidence recorded during the so-called Medieval Warm Period, or the "Little Ice Age." The Medieval Warm Period refers to an era of climate from the years A.D. 800 to 1400 believed similar to conditions in the twentieth and twenty-first centuries. The Little Ice

> "The hockey stick graph . . . is proving to be completely true. Basically the graph shows the temperatures remain consistent for 1,000 years, and then, when the industrial revolution took place, temperatures spiked."[25]
>
> — Al Gore, former U.S. vice president.

Age refers to an era of particularly cold winters that spanned from 1600 to 1850. "A casual search at any reputable library provides a wealth of information concerning these climate phenomena,"[26] insists Legates.

Indeed, Legates says, records may be spotty during those periods—particularly during the Medieval Warm Period—nevertheless, the hockey stick graph does not reflect the recorded evidence about changes in the weather during those eras. Specifically, he says, including evidence from both the Medieval Warm Period and Little Ice Age on the graph would show a modest rise in temperatures followed by a sharp dip in the pre–Industrial Age years. "Though European climate is better documented, the impacts during the Little Ice Age were widespread," says Legates. "In Argentina, Chile and southern Peru as well as southern Africa and northern China, records indicate that the last millennium began with marked warming supplanted by extreme cold during the middle centuries."[27] Clearly, he says, by including those records in the hockey stick graph, scientists would have shown that earth warmed and cooled independent of the Industrial Age.

Are the Trends Exaggerated?

Legates and other critics believe the projections made by the hockey stick graph as well as the IPCC and most other scientific papers supporting climate change have been unduly alarmist. These critics suggest that earth warmed and cooled before and that civilization is not on the path toward collapse due to fossil fuel use. "There is an exaggeration of recent trends," Legates says. "There is an underestimation of the uncertainty because they did not take into account . . . errors associated with estimating large-scale trends and temperature from observational data."[28]

The criticisms of the hockey stick graph intensified in 2009 when climate change skeptics unearthed e-mails written by several noted scientists in which the skeptics suggested that some of the evidence used to construct the hockey stick graph had been fabricated. Climate change skeptics have long charged that scientists have viewed global warming as an enormous source of income, knowing that billions of dollars would be made available by governments, private foundations, universities, and other institutions anxious to fund research. Says Patrick J. Michaels, an environmental sciences professor at the University of Virginia, "[Hundreds] of news articles [have been published] on the perils of climate change. Politicians are under pressure to act . . . [scientists] who produce the best proposals will receive the most funding. What worker-bee scientist is going to write a proposal saying that global warming is exaggerated and he doesn't need the money?"[29]

The e-mails, which were stolen, suggested that some of the faulty or misleading data helped the IPCC craft its Nobel Prize–winning report. After the e-mails were unearthed, global warming skeptics as well as others suggested a cloud is hovering over the IPCC's work. "There is a sense that something is rotten in the state of the IPCC,"[30] insisted Richard H. Moss, a senior scientist at the Joint Global Change Research Institute at the University of Maryland.

Review Finds No Wrongdoing

Several university review boards studied the case and ultimately cleared scientists of wrongdoing, finding that the errors were unintentional or misinterpreted by climate change critics. E-mails written by Mann, who helped develop the hockey stick graph, were closely examined by review boards at Penn State. Mann had been accused of using deceptive statistics—one of his e-mail exchanges with a British scientist spoke of an attempt to "hide the decline."[31] When the e-mail was made public, critics accused Mann of trying to hide a decline in global temperatures.

The term was actually used by Phillip Jones, head of the Climate Research Unit at East Anglia University in Great Britain, one of the world's leading centers for studying global warming. In a 1999 e-mail exchange with Mann, Jones discussed an analysis of tree rings that did not agree with the findings of the hockey stick graph—he felt the tree ring analysis could have been misinterpreted to reflect a mild decline in temperatures during the first half of the twentieth century. Jones was putting together his own graph at the time and discussed with Mann the importance of the tree ring data to the results. Ultimately, Jones elected to disregard the tree ring evidence, concluding that it did not provide a true picture of climate change. "I knew ultimately I'd be vindicated by a fair review of the facts," Mann said after he was cleared of wrongdoing. "Now we can all hopefully get back to doing research."[32]

Computer Models

The hockey stick graph as well as the work by Jones and other experts on global warming have not only been criticized for ignoring physical evidence but also for relying on faulty computer models. Computer modeling is a very important component of climate science as well as many other fields of study. Although written records may show that winters in the 1850s were particularly harsh, obviously nobody was recording the severity of the winters 10 million years ago. Moreover, nobody was taking readings of the carbon content of the atmosphere a million years ago or a thousand years ago or even a hundred years ago. Therefore, scientists have attempted to create computer simulations of how conditions on earth have evolved.

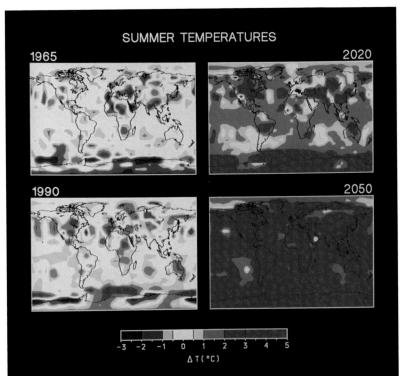

Computer-generated images show the projected increase in the world's surface air temperature to the year 2050, with red and orange indicating increased temperatures. Developed by NASA's Goddard Institute for Space Studies, these global climate models assume that greenhouse gases will continue to rise at current rates, trapping more solar radiation in the atmosphere, leading to gradual warming of the planet. Some experts debate the accuracy of these models.

The Little Ice Age

Students of European history may be familiar with the paintings of French emperor Napoleon Bonaparte leading his shivering and defeated army home through the cruel Russian winter of 1812. In fact, though, the French army began its march home in mid-October when conditions in the Russian countryside were still pleasant. The weather suddenly turned cold, and by early November the hapless French found themselves traipsing through a blizzard. By the end of November, the French soldiers were enduring temperatures recorded at -22°F (-30°C). As many as 70,000 French soldiers are believed to have died from exposure to the cold during Napoleon's retreat from Russia.

Napoleon had the misfortune to wage his campaign against Russia amid an era known as the "Little Ice Age," a period between the years 1600 and 1850 when the average temperatures were as much as 3.6°F (2°C) colder than they are today. Scientists who developed the hockey stick graph showing the trend of global warming over the past 1,000 years have been criticized for not including conditions during the Little Ice Age in the graph.

Many different details are fed into the computer to create a simulation. In addition to the carbon content of the atmosphere, scientists also speculate on the content of clouds, the amount of rainfall over time, temperature variations, wind speed, evaporation rates of the oceans and rivers, the quantity and content of pollution, and many other physical details. To create the computer models, scientists develop mathematical equations for their assumptions. When all the data is fed into the computer, the computer creates a mathematical model of the changing climate of earth.

In the relatively short time in which scientists have been creating computer models of global warming, the models have varied in their conclusions. In 1995 the IPCC adopted a computer model that declared that earth's average temperature would rise by a maximum of 10.4°F (5.8°C) by the end of the twenty-first century. Five years later the IPCC said it had adopted a revised model, which predicted the planet's temperature would rise by a maximum of 6.3°F (3.5°C). And in 2007 the IPCC modified its prediction again, this time announcing that by the end of the twenty-first century, the earth's average temperature would rise by a maximum of 11.5°F (6.4°C).

Too Much Guesswork?

The failure of these computer models to agree on their predictions has prompted critics to suggest that the science fails to provide substantial support for global warming. "The [arrogance] that can be associated with a model is amazing, because suddenly you take this sketchy understanding of a process and embody it in a model,"[33] says Warren Meyer, a Princeton University–educated aerospace engineer who has written extensively on what he regards as the faulty science behind theories of climate change. Meyer has questioned the methods used to produce computer models of climate change—he says scientists do a lot of guessing about past conditions on earth when they input the data.

The scientists who develop the computer models acknowledge that some guesswork is involved. They do not pretend to *know* the future. In fact, the computer modelers typically provide a degree of "confidence" in their models as they announce their results. Since 2001, all computer models adopted by the IPCC have been rendered with a 95 percent degree of confidence that the results are accurate. "We're never going to perfectly model reality," says Ken Fleischmann, a professor of information studies at the University of Maryland. "You let people know it's a model, it's not reality. We haven't invented a crystal ball."[34]

Taking the Many Variables into Account

Still, to many critics it does not matter how much confidence the modelers have in their work, the models are still flawed mostly because the information fed into the computer includes too many variables. In fact, computer models are designed to take many variables into account. At the National Center for Atmospheric Research in Boulder, Colorado, climate modeler Jeffrey Kiehl says that no model can account for *all* variables. Aerosol particles are one variable that might have an effect on the planet's climate. Aerosol particles include physical matter emitted into the atmosphere through combustion—cooking fires, fossil fuel burning, trash incineration, and similar types of burning.

According to Kiehl, any computer model that attempts to gauge global warming must guess at many variables involving aerosol particles. This includes not only how much has been expelled into the atmosphere but whether the particles are bright and, therefore, will reflect sunlight back into space, or whether they are dark and are more prone to absorb sunlight before it hits the surface of earth. (Soot—the byproduct of many campfires—is an example of a dark, sunlight-absorbing aerosol particles.) Aerosol particles could also cool the surface of the planet by forming clouds. With so many variables involving aerosol particles, Kiehl says, for any computer model to draw a precise conclusion about climate change would be difficult. "The more we learn [about aerosols] the less we know,"[35] says Kiehl.

Nevertheless, climate modelers stand by their work. They insist that the computer models support the physical evidence of climate change that has been gathered during the past century by James Tyndall, Guy Stewart Callendar, Charles Keeling, and the scientists who developed the hockey stick graph. "You can say, 'You know what, I don't trust the climate models, so I'm going to walk into the middle of the road with a blindfold on,'" says NASA climate scientist Gavin Schmidt. "But you know what? That's not smart."[36]

Despite their deficiencies, Kiehl says, the computer models still provide considerable evidence that earth is warming. "A number of uncertainties are still with us," Kiehl says, "but no matter what model you look at, all are producing significant warming

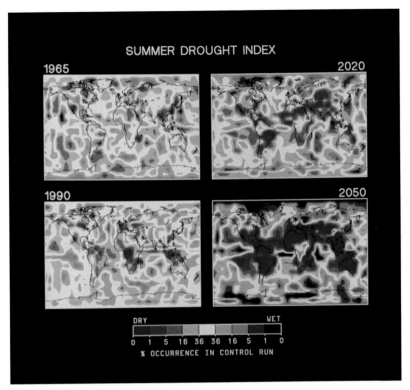

SUMMER DROUGHT INDEX

1965   2020

1990   2050

DRY   WET

0   1   5   16   36   36   16   5   1   0
% OCCURRENCE IN CONTROL RUN

Computer-generated images show the projected spread of drought up to the year 2050, with brown and orange indicating regions most likely to experience drought. Global climate models such as these, developed by NASA's Goddard Institute for Space Studies, use available data and supercomputers to model earth's climate. However, some argue that the models rely on too many assumptions.

beyond anything we've seen for 1,000 years. It's a projection that needs to be taken seriously."[37]

Profiting from Fossil Fuels

As computer modelers as well as scientists defend their work, they are quick to point out that much of the rhetoric that has been raised against them has its roots in interest groups that profit from a continuing use of fossil fuels. For example, one of the most vocal organizations that questioned the science supporting global warming was the Global Climate Coalition. In the early 1990s, as science started producing important climate change studies, the coalition asserted, "The role of greenhouse gases in climate change is not well understood."[38]

The coalition was established by a number of private companies and trade associations representing the oil and coal industries as well as the automotive industry, which is heavily reliant on the continued use of gasoline-fueled engines. Records showed that in 1997, as delegates from some 200 nations were negotiating the terms of the Kyoto Protocol, a treaty designed to limit carbon emissions, the coalition was provided with a budget of $1.7 billion by its sponsors, who expected it to spend that money debunking the science supporting climate change.

Even as the coalition campaigned against the Kyoto Protocol, though, documents that surfaced in 2009 revealed that its scientists were telling the organization's leaders that climate change was directly attributable to fossil fuel use. "The scientific basis for the greenhouse effect and the potential impact of human emissions of greenhouse gases such as carbon dioxide on climate is well established and cannot be denied," wrote the coalition's scientists in an internal report. "Contrarian theories [about climate change] raise interesting questions about our total understanding of the climate process, but they do not offer convincing arguments against the conventional model of greenhouse gas emission-induced climate change."[39] The panel of scientists that wrote the report was headed by Leonard S. Bernstein, a chemical engineer employed by Exxon-Mobil, one of the world's largest oil companies.

Deception and Disinformation?

The documents show that even though the coalition was told by its own scientists that climate change is caused by greenhouse gas emissions, the group continued its efforts to debunk the work of the IPCC as well as other individuals, universities, and foundations performing serious climate change science. Benjamin D. Santer, a climate scientist for the Lawrence Livermore National Laboratory in California who helped write the IPCC study, said it was clear from the Global Climate Coalition's own experts that the IPCC report was based on sound science. The problem was that the science did not support the business goals of the coalition's sponsors, which is to sell more oil and coal. "I'm amazed and astonished that the Global Climate Coalition had in their possession scientific information that substantiated our cautious findings and then chose to suppress that information,"[40] Santer said.

British environmental activist George Monbiot added that supporting the truth about climate change was never in the interest of the Global Climate Coalition. "They didn't have to win the argument to succeed," he said, "only to cause as much confusion as possible."[41]

The Global Climate Coalition disbanded in 2002, but its work is being carried on by such organizations as the American Petroleum Institute (API), the trade association for American oil companies. In fact, the API has continued financing scientific studies that have suggested global warming is not caused by greenhouse gas emissions. One study financed by the API, published in the journal *Energy and the Environment*, suggests that the temperature change during the Medieval Warm Period was a lot more severe than previously believed, thus providing proof that global warming occurred during an era when most of the carbon emitted into the atmosphere was generated by primitive cooking fires.

Given the oil industry money behind the study, environmentalists believe readers would do well to be wary of the article's conclusions. Said Ross Gelbspan, whose 1997 book *The Heat Is On* called attention to efforts by the oil industry to discredit climate science, "The contradictory statements of a tiny handful of discredited scientists, funded by big coal and big oil, represent a deliberate—and extremely reckless—campaign of deception and disinformation."[42]

> "I'm amazed and astonished that the Global Climate Coalition had in their possession scientific information that substantiated our cautious findings and then chose to suppress that information."[40]
>
> — Benjamin D. Santer, climate scientist for the Lawrence Livermore National Laboratory in California.

Scientists Stand by Their Work

The work by groups such as the Global Climate Coalition aside, still remaining are some reasons to question the science that suggests global warming is caused by the human activity of burning fossil fuels. Even some of the professionals who create the computer-generated models of earth's future climate admit that a lot of guesswork is involved.

And yet, many scientists stand by their work. They have accumulated physical evidence in places like the Tibetan Plateau, relying on high-tech processes that include satellite imagery and global positioning systems. Moreover, their work is being followed very closely by national governments that have an interest in protecting the lives and homes of their citizens. These scientists say they are at least 95 percent confident that their predictions are sound.

Facts

- According to U.S. senator James Inhofe of Oklahoma, more than 700 scientists disagree with the conclusions of the UN Intergovernmental Panel on Climate Change, which found that global warming is caused by the human activity of burning fossil fuels.

- Three separate boards of scientists in Great Britain reviewed the e-mails written by East Anglia University climate scientist Phillip Jones; each panel concluded that Jones did not fabricate evidence of global warming.

- Released in 1998, the first hockey stick graph traced global warming back to the year A.D. 1000; in 2003, Pennsylvania State University professor Michael Mann extended the graph back to the year A.D. 200 and drew the same conclusion—that the climate of earth was stable until the Industrial Age.

- According to scientists who have studied the Tibetan Plateau, unless the region's loss of glacial ice is slowed, India will lack 50 percent of the water it needs by 2030.

- Thirty-two percent of Americans believe global warming will affect them in their lifetime, according to a 2010 Gallup poll; in 2008 a similar poll found that 40 percent of Americans believed they would be affected by global warming within their lifetimes.

- The hockey stick graph estimated that the difference in average temperatures between the Medieval Warm Period and Little Ice Age is about 0.5°F (0.3°C). A subsequent study by Swiss climate researchers suggested the difference in average temperatures between the two eras was four times greater than the hockey stick graph estimated.

CHAPTER THREE

What Are the Potential Economic Impacts of Climate Change?

P eter Timofeeff is largely unknown in the United States, but the meteorologist is a well-recognized celebrity in the Netherlands. Each evening, millions of Dutch citizens tune in to Dutch TV to watch Timofeeff forecast the weather.

Because Timofeeff is so well-known and respected in the Netherlands, the Dutch government enlisted him to appear in a number of public service commercials intended to draw people's attention to the dangers of climate change. The ads are mostly humorous—but they do deliver a serious message. In one commercial, Timofeeff relaxes on a beach chair as sea water slowly engulfs him. Behind Timofeeff, a child building a sand castle abandons his labors in panic, but Timofeeff, oblivious to the truth, continues to relax in the sunshine even as the water rises above his waist. In another TV ad, Timofeeff steps into a bathtub, fully clothed. As he turns on the shower, dousing himself, he says, "These are our rivers. The climate is changing. It will rain more often, and more heavily."[43]

Residents of the Netherlands fear that rising sea levels resulting from climate change will drown their country, half of which lies either below or just above sea level. The Dutch island of Marken, whose harbor is pictured here, is among the areas at risk.

Much to Fear

In fact, the Dutch believe they have much to fear from climate change. A quarter of the Netherlands lies below sea level. Another quarter of the country is just slightly above sea level—still low enough to be endangered should waters from the North Sea rise or the Rhine and Meuse rivers overflow their banks. Many scientists and political leaders in the Netherlands believe that unless steps are taken to slow climate change, by the end of the twenty-first century the dramatic rise in sea levels has the potential to bring widespread destruction to the Netherlands. They believe the rising waters will submerge half the nation, destroying tens of thousands of homes, businesses, factories, farms, highways, and other infrastructure. Millions of Dutch citizens could be left homeless and unemployed.

That is why the Dutch government has undertaken a massive public works program, known as "Room for the River," to buy up farmland that borders the nation's rivers. The program is expected to cost hundreds of millions of dollars. In the event of flooding, the government would direct the overflowing waters away from populated areas and toward farmland. Such action, officials say, would prevent irreparable damage to buildings and infrastructure. However, the steep expense has prompted many climate change skeptics in the Netherlands to question the project. "Some people don't get it," shrugs Eelke Turkstra, head of the Room for the River program. "They think this project is stupid. But I think it is stupid to continue in the old way."[44]

Strains on the Economy

Environmentalists believe that climate change, hastened by continued fossil fuel use, will have a devastating effect on the global economy. They argue, for example, that as earth grows warmer the likelihood of bad storms, particularly hurricanes, increases. Hurricanes cause destruction over a wide swath of territory, often costing billions of dollars in lost homes, businesses, roads, bridges, and other infrastructure. Edward Cameron, an official at the World Bank who examines the impact of climate change, says such storms have already grown in intensity and have proved to be particularly destructive to the small island states of the Caribbean. He says,

> In 2004 Grenada, an island considered to be outside the hurricane belt, was devastated when Hurricane Ivan struck, destroying over 90 percent of the country's infrastructure and housing stock and causing over $800 million in damages, the equivalent of 200 percent of Grenada's [annual economy]. The increase in frequency and intensity of these storms expected due to climate change could well place further strain on political, social and economic systems and act as an additional constraint on development in the region.[45]

Elsewhere on the planet, the Chinese already believe weather patterns caused by global warming have impacted life in their country. China typically experiences strong monsoon winds that drive the weather across the country. In recent years, Chinese meteorologists have found that the monsoon winds are weaker than in the past. As a result, China's coastal regions are receiving more rainfall and flooding more often, while the interior of the country is prone to drought.

In 2010 heavy rains hit northeast China, swelling the Yangtze River. Some 300 miles downstream, the city of Wuhan was hit with massive flooding. More than 1,400 people died in the flooding, which caused $26 billion in damage. Said Jiang Gaoming, chief researcher at the Chinese Academy of Sciences' Institute of Botany, "Many experts attribute this year's flood to climate anomalies. It sounds right, since the precipitation in the Yangtze River valley this year was extremely high, and global warming might have contributed to the high precipitation."[46]

California Grape Growers May Suffer

Hurricanes and other major storms cause economic havoc virtually overnight, but economists believe that climate change can also have a gradual impact on people's lives over the course of many years. For example, due to climate change the high quality of California wines is expected to change dramatically within a few decades.

The quality of grapes used in wines is greatly affected by temperature—grapes grown in warmer regions are less acidic, providing a less tart taste to the wines they make. People who enjoy California wines look for that tartness. Grapes grown in the cooler climate of California's Napa Valley, north of San Francisco, currently fetch more than $4,000 a ton (0.9 metric tons). Just 150 miles (241km) south, in the state's sun-parched Central Valley, grapes are sold for $260 a ton. The average temperature in the Central Valley is 5°F (2.8°C) warmer than the average temperature in the Napa Valley.

As the climate of the Napa Valley warms, some grape growers believe they will be forced to find other places to grow grapes—a notion they find highly undesirable given the international reputation that has been earned by Napa wines. "Wine is tied to place more than any other form of agriculture, in the sense that the names of the place are on the bottle," says David Graves, a veteran Napa Valley grape grower. "If traditional sugar-beet growing regions in eastern Colorado had

to move north, nobody would care. But if wine grapes can't grow in the Napa Valley anymore—which is an extreme statement, but let's say so for the sake of argument—suddenly you have a global warming poster child right up there with the polar bears."[47]

Chinese shop owners try to salvage their goods from a flooded market along the Yangtze River. Heavy rains swelled the river in 2010, causing severe flooding. The Chinese believe weather patterns caused by global warming are to blame.

Inaction May Hurt the Economy

In 2009 the federal government released a report on the potential economic consequences of climate change in America. Titled *Global Climate Change Impacts in the United States*, the report paints a dim picture of life in America should temperatures continue to rise. "What we've shown in this assessment is that we do need to act sooner rather than later," said Donald Wuebbles, an atmospheric scientist at the University of Illinois and a chief author of the report. "We want to avoid the worst of the kind of changes that we looked at."[48]

According to the report, agriculture and food production will be challenged due to the increased number of heat waves, stresses on crops caused by too much rain, and the growth of insect populations that are common during moist conditions. In addition to food shortages, the report also said a number of other problems would occur. For example, the report said, medical resources of the country will be taxed, mostly by heat-related illnesses that are expected to increase six-fold by the end of the twenty-first century. Such illnesses and the death rates associated with them will also put a strain on the labor market as well as the insurance industry.

Also, as the Dutch have already recognized, the report said that governments must address the likelihood that rivers would overflow their banks, flooding cities and other areas. Constant flooding could disrupt transportation if streets and highways, railroads, tunnels, bridges, and airports are swamped under water. Says the report, "While it is widely recognized that emissions from transportation have a major impact on climate, climate change will also have a major impact on transportation."[49]

The recreation and tourism industries could be devastated—beaches could be washed away while ski slopes are turned to slush. "In our back yards, climate change is happening, and it's happening now," said Jane Lubchenco, administrator of the National Oceanic and Atmospheric Administration, which contributed to the report. "It's not too late to act. Decisions made now will determine whether we get big changes or small ones."[50]

An Inaccurate Picture

Climate change skeptics believe the report does not paint an accurate picture of future life in the United States. For starters, aerospace engineer Warren Meyer says agriculture will not be under stress during warmer climate periods but, rather, is likely to thrive. Meyer points out that during the Medieval Warm Period, the expansion of earth's population could not have occurred unless farmers of the era met the demand for food. Clearly, he says, the warmer conditions during this era were beneficial for crops. In the future, Meyer predicts, similarly warm conditions could also enhance the growth of crops. Moreover, Meyer points out, one of history's worst eras of famine and plague occurred in the era following the Medieval Warm Period—the Little Ice Age—a time when earth's temperature is said to have cooled. Indeed, an epidemic of bubonic plague, which wiped out 15 percent of the population of London, England, in 1665 and 1666, occurred within the era of the Little

> "Many experts attribute this year's flood to climate anomalies. It sounds right, since the precipitation in the Yangtze River valley this year was extremely high, and global warming might have contributed to the high precipitation."[46]
>
> — Jiang Gaoming, chief researcher at the Chinese Academy of Sciences' Institute of Botany.

Ice Age. "The Medieval Warm Period in Europe was a time of expanding populations driven by increasing harvests," says Meyer. "When the Medieval Warm Period ended and decades of cooler weather ensued, the Great Famine resulted—a famine which many blame for weakening the population and making later plague outbreaks more severe."[51]

Skiing Where There Is No Snow

Few people stand to be more affected by a warmer earth than the people who own ski resorts or are employed by the resorts. Skiing is big business in places like Colorado, New England, and many European countries where tourists fuel the local economies. In Colorado alone, the ski industry is a $2 billion a year business, employing some 8 percent of all workers in the state. Meanwhile, in Vermont the skiing industry employs some 12,000 people, while in New Hampshire, the sport contributes nearly $600 million to the state's economy.

In the ski resort town of Aspen, Colorado, Auden Schendler, who manages two local ski slopes, says he started noticing business picking up about 10 years ago. Schendler says the increased tourism in Aspen was due to shorter ski seasons in Europe. Schendler says the European ski lodges were hit first because they tend to be located lower in the mountains at elevations of about 6,000 feet (1,829m) or 8,000 feet (2,438m). In America, most western ski resorts are located at elevations of about 11,000 feet (3,353m).

Now, though, Schendler says the warmer conditions have caught up with Aspen. "More balmy Novembers, more rainy Marches," Schendler says. "That's what we're seeing, and that's what the science suggests would happen. If you graph frost-free days, there are more and more in the last 30 years."

Quoted in Clive Thompson, "Betting on Change," *Slate,* April 19, 2010. www.slate.com.

Other portions of the report have also been attacked. William Gray, a professor of atmospheric science at Colorado State University, has spent his entire career studying hurricanes and is convinced they are not caused by warmer temperatures sparked by greenhouse gas emissions. Gray acknowledges that earth is currently going through a brief warming phase—and that the rising temperature of the oceans has occasionally spawned severe storms. He insists, though, that the warming of the oceans is part of a natural cycle and not caused by carbon emissions. "Few people know what I know," Gray says. "I've been in the tropics. I've flown in airplanes into storms. I've done studies of convection, cloud clusters and how the moist process works. I don't think anybody in the world understands how the atmosphere functions better than me. . . . I don't think this warming period of the last 30 years can keep on going. It may warm another three, five, eight years, and then it will start to cool."[52]

Solutions May Hurt the Economy

Gray and other climate change skeptics worry that if political leaders are pressured into enacting laws that would cut carbon emissions, the economic fallout could be devastating to both industrialized and developing countries. "The globe has many serious environmental problems," says Gray. "Most of these problems are regional or local in nature, not global. Forced global reductions in human-produced greenhouse gases will not offer much benefit for the globe's serious regional and local environmental problems. . . . We need a prosperous economy to have sufficient resources to further adapt and expand energy production."[53]

Indeed, Gray and other critics point out that industrialized and developing economies cannot suddenly cut back on the use of oil and coal. In a world that was still struggling to free itself from a massive economic recession in 2010, these experts argue that even slight cutbacks in fossil fuel use would be devastating—leading to massive unemployment, poverty, and many other social ills. Says Sallie Baliunas, a Harvard University astrophysicist,

The economic impact of significantly cutting fossil fuel use will be hard-felt, and [it] will be devastating to those on fixed incomes, those in developing countries, and those on the margins of the economy. For the next several decades, fossil fuel use is key to improving the human condition. . . . Fossil fuels have been used for many economic, health, and environmental benefits. But the environmental catastrophes that have been forecast from their use have yet to be demonstrated by their critics.[54]

Worldwide Fuel Consumption

Statistics show that each day the worldwide consumption of fossil fuels is enormous. According to the Paris, France–based International Energy Agency (IEA), consumers across the globe burn some 85 million barrels of oil a day. Since a barrel of oil typically produces about 20 gallons (76L) of gasoline, it means consumers are burning through 1.7 billion gallons (6.4 billion L) of gasoline a day.

Today, people no longer keep coal boilers in their basements, and ships and locomotives no longer run on coal, but coal remains an important source of energy. Coal-fired plants make 42 percent of the world's electricity (the rest is made largely by nuclear power plants). Although nuclear power is a highly efficient source of energy, construction of nuclear plants often cost billions of dollars; moreover, many safety issues surround nuclear power. As such, few nuclear power plants are expected to go into operation over the next several decades. Therefore, the IEA predicts, electric utilities will be relying more on coal in the near future—by 2030, the agency predicts, coal will make 44 percent of the world's electricity.

Of the three main fossil fuels, natural gas is regarded as the cleanest, meaning its use gives off less carbon than coal and oil. Still, worldwide consumption of natural gas is enormous. According to the U.S. Department of Energy, worldwide consumers use 302 billion cubic feet (8.6 billion cubic m) of natural gas per day. It takes about 60 cubic feet (1.7 cubic m) of natural gas to heat the typical home on a day when the outside temperature is 20°F (-7°C).

"The economic impact of significantly cutting fossil fuel use will be hard-felt, and [it] will be devastating to those on fixed incomes, those in developing countries, and those on the margins of the economy."[54]

— Sallie Baliunas, Harvard University astrophysicist.

The Oil and Gas Economy

Transportation, electricity, and sources of heat are largely dependent on fossil fuels, but fossil fuels are also employed in uses other than those that are energy-related. Many plastics, fertilizers, cosmetics, paints, and other products are oil-based and represent a significant sector of the economy. Industry leaders insist that the environmental impacts of global warming remain unproven, and therefore cutting back on fossil fuel use would cause more economic damage than climate change is purported to cost. Says a statement by the American Petroleum Institute, "The oil and natural gas industry is the backbone of the American economy. What happens in the industry is felt throughout the entire economy. The oil and natural gas industry not only provides most of the energy that heats our homes, powers our factories and offices, and gets Americans to school and work, it also supports 9.2 million American jobs and adds more than $1 trillion to the national economy. That's 7.5 percent of our nation's wealth."[55]

Al Gore and other environmentalists counter, though, that fossil fuels have often caused some of the most devastating economic downturns in American history. For example, in 1973, after the United States backed Israel in a war against Egypt, Syria, and Jordan, angry Arab oil ministers imposed an embargo on oil shipments to the United States. The embargo lasted for six months, a time in which many Americans were forced to wait in long lines to buy gasoline. Before the embargo, gasoline cost an average of about 40 cents a gallon (4.5L). During the embargo, the price of gasoline shot up to more than a dollar a gallon—and never came down.

More recently, many economists believe that a jump in oil prices in 2008 touched off the recession that eventually led to widespread unemployment that was still being felt in America and other countries through 2010. (In January 2007 the price of oil on the world market stood at roughly $46 a barrel; by June 2008 the price had jumped to more than $126 a barrel.) When oil and coal become more expensive, industries find themselves with less money to expand, develop new products, or hire workers. "The drops in spending caused by the oil price increases resulted in lost incomes and jobs in affected sectors, with those losses then magnifying other stresses on the economy and producing a . . . dynamic

Climate Refugees

Food shortages caused by global warming could force as many as 1 billion people to leave their homes by 2050, according to the Earth Institute, a New York–based aid agency. "Human-induced climate . . . change is likely to make many parts of the world uninhabitable, or at least uneconomic," says Jeffrey Sachs, director of the institute. "Over the course of a few decades, if not sooner, hundreds of millions of people may be compelled to relocate."

Hardest hit may be Africa, which could lose two-thirds of its arable land due to desertification, which occurs when croplands lose their ability to produce vegetation and turn into deserts. Desertification occurs when insufficient rain falls in a region. Although many scientists expect climate change to result in more rainfall because the atmosphere holds more moisture, some areas could experience droughts because rainfall is sporadic or falls in concentrations in some places but misses others. Also, desertification could occur because warmer temperatures draw moisture out of the soil.

When regions can no longer produce food, people will be forced to move to other areas—crowding out others and taxing the local food and water supplies. As such, they become "climate refugees." Said Thomas Downing, director of the Stockholm, Sweden–based Environment Institute, "There is going to be a lot of population movement linked to climate. . . . When you add climate to other forces that push people beyond the capacity to cope, the numbers will increase."

Quoted in Brad Knickerbocker, "Warming May Uproot Millions," *Christian Science Monitor*, June 21, 2007, p. 10.

that gathered force," says University of California at San Diego economics professor James D. Hamilton. "The economic downturn of 2007–2008 should be added to the list of recessions to which oil prices appear to have made a material contribution."[56]

Steam clouds pour from the cooling towers of a coal-fired power plant in Germany. The International Energy Agency predicts that 44 percent of the world's electricity will come from coal by 2030.

Today gasoline often costs $3 or more a gallon (4.5L), and prices are controlled to a large extent by the Organization of Petroleum Exporting Countries (OPEC), a cartel of 13 nations that produce nearly 40 percent of the world's oil supply. Some of those nations, including Libya, Iran, and Venezuela, have maintained hostile relations with the United States.

Concerns About Economic Stability

Therefore, Gore says, since a large share of America's oil is imported from unfriendly nations in the Middle East and elsewhere, America's reliance on fossil fuels hardly provides economic stability. Says Gore, "If you want your energy bills to go up, you should support an ever greater dependence on foreign oil, because the rate of new discoveries is declining as demand in China and India is growing, and the price of oil and thus the price of coal will go sky high. That is the formula for increasing energy bills."[57]

To truly spur the economy, Gore urges homeowners and industries to invest in wind, solar, and other alternative energy projects.

At this point, according to the U.S. Department of Energy, just 7 percent of the energy in America is provided by renewable sources. Gore says millions of homes and businesses can be outfitted with solar panels, wind turbines, and geothermal heating devices, which draw heat from within the earth. Such projects, he says, would help spark billions of dollars of investment in retrofitting homes and businesses. Moreover, none of those energy sources emit a single molecule of carbon dioxide into the atmosphere—a factor that would help slow climate change. And once those systems are installed, they continue making power from sunlight, wind, or the earth at no cost to the owner. "All forms of energy are expensive," says Gore, "but over time, renewable energy gets cheaper, while carbon-based energy gets more expensive. Unlike carbon-based fuels, the wind and the sun and the Earth itself provide fuel that is free in amounts that are effectively limitless."[58]

A Debate About the Economy

The debate over climate change often comes down to a debate about the economy. On one side, many scientists and environmental activists predict a gloomy period ahead if steps are not taken to rein in fossil fuel emissions. They believe that severe storms could wipe out cities while rising rivers submerge homes. They fear that diseases would spread, taxing the ability of doctors and hospitals to care for the sick. Many activists predict worldwide food shortages caused by stresses on agricultural land. In the Netherlands, officials are taking no chances—they are preparing for a very warm, and wet, future.

Skeptics are not so sure. Scientists like Gray concede that storms in recent years have been more severe. Gray, however, does not see cutbacks on greenhouse gas emissions having any effect on the number or severity of the storms. Warren Meyer points out that over the course of history, people have been healthier and food more abundant in periods of warmer temperatures. And many experts argue that cutting back on fossil fuels would have a devastating impact on the world's economy by slowing industrial growth and derailing important modes of transportation that shuttle goods to the market and workers to their jobs.

Facts

- Beluga Shipping, a German company, has added $600,000 a year to its profits by shipping goods to Russia across Arctic passages that were previously closed by ice; before the passages opened, the goods had to be shipped thousands of extra miles through the Suez Canal.

- Catastrophic weather events, such as hurricanes and floods, caused $200 billion in damages in 2008; it was the third highest total for such losses on record.

- Profits for Pentair Inc., a Minnesota company, have soared to more than $3 billion a year. Pentair makes huge pumps used to siphon floodwaters away from populated areas.

- The California State Teachers' Retirement System, which provides pensions to retired California teachers, refuses to invest in companies that contribute to global warming. The organization controls assets of more than $130 billion.

- According to the report *Global Climate Change Impacts in the United States*, one area of the economy that would be hit hard by climate change is oil production—30 percent of the nation's oil is produced by offshore oil rigs in the Gulf of Mexico. The rigs would be under constant barrage by hurricanes in a warmer world.

- Scientists at Lawrence Livermore National Laboratory in California predict that warmer temperatures will cause a 20 percent decline in almond and walnut crops over the next 40 years.

- European ski resorts have started adding artificial snow to their slopes. The snow is composed of similar materials used to make artificial turf for athletic fields.

What Are the Potential Environmental Impacts of Climate Change?

While many scientists warn that global warming could lead to melting polar ice and loss of species native to colder climates such as polar bears, penguins, and seals, other scientists have found evidence of climate change in much different environments. They believe that warmer temperatures in the planet's oceans have caused widespread destruction to coral colonies and therefore, to coral reefs. These colorful reefs are composed of the calcium exoskeletons of these tiny marine animals.

Concerns About Coral Reefs

Coral is found mostly in tropical climates. The largest coral reef in the world is the Great Barrier Reef, which stretches across some 1,600 miles (2,575km) of ocean floor off the coast of Australia. Studies of the reef have found that it is in decline, breaking apart as the population of corals declines. Scientists blame climate change. They say that the rising temperature of the ocean water has been killing off algae, which serves as a source of food for coral colonies. Moreover, scientists worry about other marine wildlife that live in

The largest coral reef in the world, Australia's Great Barrier Reef (pictured), is in decline. Scientists say climate change is to blame for rising ocean temperatures that have killed algae, the primary source of food for coral colonies.

close proximity to the reef's ecosystem. These animals include fish that feed on the coral as well as crustaceans and mollusks that live in the reef.

This wildlife, in turn, draws in marine predators such as sharks, eels, skates, and rays that also rely on coral reefs to sustain their species. In other words, coral reefs are an important part of the ocean's ecosystem. Without them, the food chain would be interrupted, which would lead to the loss of many ocean species. One study of the coral reefs found near the Seychelles islands in the Indian Ocean has identified four species of fish that may be extinct due to the decline in the reefs. Says Australian marine biologist Charlie Veron,

> The future is horrific. There is no hope of reefs surviving to even mid-century in any form that we now recognize. If, and when, they go, they will take with them about one-third of the world's marine biodiversity. Then there is a domino effect, as reefs fail so will other ecosystems. This is the path of a mass extinction event, when most life, especially tropical marine life, goes extinct.[59]

Others insist that the evidence does not support the loss of the coral reefs. Geologist Ian Plimer says that coral has managed to survive on earth for at least 500 million years during periods in which the temperatures of the planet's oceans were higher than they are now. "If sea surface temperature increases and sea level rises, the reef will keep pace as it has done in the past," he says. "Over the last 500 million years, corals have survived in much warmer and much cooler waters."[60]

Threats to Polar Bears

While political leaders, economists, and atmospheric experts debate whether hurricanes and crop losses are caused by climate change, environmental activists contend an even clearer example of the adverse effects of global warming exists. That example is species loss—not only in tropical waters where coral reefs are affected, but in virtually every corner of the planet. Says NASA's Gavin Schmidt,

> Climate change is either leaving them no place to move to or, especially if they are sedentary, changing too fast for them to adapt and survive. An estimate of potential rates of extinction . . . implies that 15 to 37 percent of . . . 1,103 species examined will be on the road to extinction by 2050. Based on this study, some have speculated that perhaps a million or more of the Earth's species could face similar fates.[61]

The one place where climate change seems to be making the most impact is in the Arctic, where environmentalists believe the future of polar bears is very much in doubt. In 2008 the U.S. Fish and Wildlife Service listed polar bears as members of a "threatened" species, meaning they are considered vulnerable to extinction in the near future.

For polar bears, ice is a natural habitat—they spend their entire lives on ice. When the ice retreats, their habitats decline. To survive, if the ice is receding, the bears would be forced to head north; therefore, they would be squeezed into smaller areas. Andrew Derocher, a University of Alberta biologist, says reducing the amount of Arctic ice affects polar bears the same way cutting down large swaths of forests would affect deer, birds, squirrels, mice, toads, snakes, and all manner of other critters that live in woodlands. It would deprive them of their natural habitat and make the remaining habitat, where they would have to compete for declining sources of food, much more crowded. "That's essentially what you're doing when you take away the sea ice," he says. "If you have an erosion of the bears' habitat, you'll see the populations erode and retreat northwards."[62]

Conflicting Facts

As with many issues involving climate change, critics suggest the fears of polar bear extinction are overblown. Many contend that rather than facing extinction, the populations of polar bears have been increasing in recent decades—proof that some species native to the Arctic are thriving. Mitchell Taylor, a Canadian biologist and expert on polar bears, was commissioned by the government of the Nunavut Territory in northern Canada to inventory the polar bear population in the region of the Davis Strait, a 54,000-square-mile area (139,860 square km) of the Atlantic Ocean that lies between the territory and Greenland. Taylor estimated that a polar bear population of 850 recorded in the mid-1980s has grown to more than 2,100 bears today. "Of the 13 populations of polar bears in Canada, 11 are stable or increasing in number," Taylor said. "They are not going extinct, or even appear to be affected at present. It is just silly to predict the demise of polar bears in 25 years based on [climate change] hysteria."[63]

Critics of Taylor's inventory suggested, though, that the results are tainted by the interests of the Nunavut government, which is dominated by the Inuit who want to keep the polar bears off endangered species lists. The Inuit often hunt the bears, which have been known to attack human settlements near the Davis Strait. "I don't think there is any question polar bears are in danger from global warming," said Derocher. "People who deny that have a clear interest in hunting bears."[64]

"The future is horrific. There is no hope of reefs surviving to even mid-century in any form that we now recognize."[59]

— Charlie Veron, Australian marine biologist.

How Do Coral Reefs Die?

Scientists can tell when coral reefs die—they turn white. This process is known as "bleaching." Coral reefs get their color from algae, the tiny plants that provide food for the coral polyps. The relationship is symbiotic—the coral polyps living in the reef feed on the algae while providing nutrients for the growth of the algae. When the algae die, the reef loses its color and turns white. As the coral dies, the reefs often deteriorate and break apart.

Bleaching has been attributed to many factors, such as disease and pollution, but many scientists believe climate change is a major factor—the algae are unable to survive in warmer waters. Nineteen percent of the world's coral reefs are believed to have died in recent years, and another 15 percent are projected to die within the next 20 years.

Scientists fear that the decay of coral reefs will lead to an interruption in the aquatic food chain—other marine life drawn to food in the coral reefs will die as well. "You could argue that a complete collapse of the marine ecosystem would be one of the consequences of losing corals," says biologist Kent Carpenter of Old Dominion University in Virginia. "You're going to have a tremendous cascade effect for all life in the oceans."

Quoted in Brian Skoloff, "Imagining the Seas with No Coral Reefs," *Philadelphia Inquirer*, March 31, 2010.

The Climate Change Trigger

While the experts debate the size of the world's polar bear population, other scientists believe that other species are under stress due to climate change in places that are not very cold. Many thousands of miles away from the Davis Strait, scientists in Central America and South America have studied wildlife populations and concluded that global warming has helped wipe out more than 70 different species of frogs. The frogs are known as harlequin frogs and, because of their thin skins, are susceptible to acquiring coats of fungi.

One specific fungus, known as chytrid, is known to breed diseases that can be fatal to frogs. Because of warmer temperatures, the fungus is more prevalent in the frogs' habitat. After studying frog populations, scientists at the Monteverde Cloud Forest Preserve in Costa Rica determined that several species of harlequin frogs had been wiped out by the disease-carrying fungus. "Disease is the bullet killing frogs, but climate change is pulling the trigger," said the preserve's resident scientist, J. Alan Pounds. "Global warming is wreaking havoc on amphibians and will cause staggering losses of biodiversity if we don't do something fast."[65]

Searching for Other Places to Live

When animals such as polar bears or frogs are affected by changing conditions, their natural responses are often to find other places to live. As they move from place to place, they often find themselves in competition with the animals whose territories they have invaded. According to Schmidt, a recent study of more than 1,600 different species of animals found that about half have shifted their habitats to other places in the past 140 years. Many of these species are fish that live in cold water. As their habitats have warmed, Schmidt says, the marine animals have moved further north, where they compete with native fish for available food. Eventually, he predicts, the fish will go as far north as they possibly can—then run out of new places to live.

Meanwhile, he says, on land many species of lizards have been moving up mountains as conditions below become intolerable for them. Eventually, Schmidt says, these lizards will reach the top of the mountains—and have no place else to go. "There is less area at the tops of hemispheres and the tops of mountains, so eventually, as warming continues, the preferred habitats of some species will completely disappear,"[66] he says.

Displaced Animals May Endanger Humans

Sometimes, animals looking for new places to live encroach on places where people live. In some parts of Russia villagers have noticed brown bears wandering into rural towns. The reason is that the bears are hibernating for shorter periods because winters are shorter. Having gotten less sleep, the bears are grumpy and hungry—and dangerous. Russian officials have warned rural villagers to stay away from the bears.

Meanwhile, every year about 30,000 people who swim in the Mediterranean Sea are stung by jellyfish. Jellyfish attacks used to be far less common, but scientists say the rise in water temperatures along the Spanish, Italian, and North African coasts have drawn the jellyfish toward the beaches.

As the examples of the Russian bears and Mediterranean jellyfish illustrate, when animals leave their natural habits they could pose dangers to humans—and not only by attacking them. Animals often carry diseases or parasites that spread diseases. These diseases can cross over into the human population when animals encroach into human habitats. In Australia, a southern migration of bats drawn to warmer climates is believed responsible for spreading many diseases, including Hendra virus, which can be fatal. Already, human fatalities have been reported. "They are shifting in a southerly direction and the black [bat] can be found as far as Melbourne as the climate becomes warmer due to climate change. So, the potential for [outbreaks of] any disease carried by the bats, such as the Hendra virus, goes with them," says biologist Lesley Hughes of Macquarie University in Sydney, Australia. "Climate change is affecting the distribution of lots of species and bats are strong flyers and are moving faster than we had expected them to."[67]

Also of concern are insects that carry disease, particularly mosquitoes. According to the World Health Organization (WHO), malaria epidemics in Kenya, Rwanda, and Tanzania are directly attributable to larger than normal mosquito populations, which WHO believes are caused by warmer and longer summers—the peak period for mosquito growth. Says Schmidt, "Invasive species are becoming more problematic as climate change favors their success."[68]

Baseball and Climate Change

Insects do not only spread disease that can endanger humans, they also spread diseases responsible for destroying crops, trees, and other plants. The abundance of pine bark beetles has been

"If sea surface temperature increases and sea level rises, the reef will keep pace as it has done in the past. Over the last 500 million years, corals have survived in much warmer and much cooler waters."[60]

— Ian Plimer, Australian geologist.

A Kenyan woman pulls aside the netting that protects her sleeping children from malaria-carrying mosquitoes. Health officials say malaria epidemics in Kenya and other African countries have resulted from extended mosquito-breeding seasons brought on by warmer and longer summers.

of particular concern to scientists. Due to longer, warmer, and moister conditions, populations of these beetles have increased in recent years. As their name suggests, they feed on the bark of pine trees. According to Schmidt, up to 90 percent of the pine trees in Colorado have been attacked by pine bark beetles, with many trees dying as a result.

Another tree that is believed to have been harmed by larger populations of pests is the ash tree, which has been victimized by a beetle known as the emerald ash borer. The beetle is believed responsible for killing some 25 million ash trees in Michigan, Illinois, Ohio, and Maryland. Authorities believe the future of the American ash tree is in peril—in Michigan, state officials have collected and stored seeds from ash trees in case the species is completely wiped out. Moreover, authorities concede that no one knows how to kill the beetles before they destroy all the ash trees. "It just doesn't look good," said Daniel Herms, an associate professor of entomology at Ohio State University. "The current technology won't be able to stop it."[69]

The ash tree serves a very significant purpose in American culture: Most baseball bats are made out of ash. If the ash tree disappears from the American landscape, climate change could be responsible for causing a significant change in an important tradition of the sport. Many bat makers have already started using other woods, such as maple and birch, while youth leagues continue to use aluminum bats. Still, many baseball purists find unacceptable the notion that the sport would eventually be played without bats made of ash. "The bug is definitely a threat to the ash population, and the whole bat industry in general would change if the ash is lost,"[70] said Mike Gregory, vice president of BWP Bats, which makes about 40,000 ash bats a year, including about 13,000 used by Major League players.

Failure to Adapt

Many climate change skeptics do not deny that species are disappearing from the planet. Bjørn Lomborg acknowledges that thousands of species representing all manner of living things—plants, insects, mammals, reptiles, fish—have been disappearing for many centuries. In the view of Lomborg and other skeptics, though, these species have not disappeared from the planet because their environments grew warmer. Rather, they went extinct because they failed to adapt to changing environments—which has been true for all extinct species on earth for millions of years.

Over the course of the life of the planet, tens of millions of species have likely come and gone. Some scientists have estimated that as much as 95 percent of life on the planet has passed into extinction over the course of the past 250 million years, with the typical species lasting between 1 million and 10 million years. Therefore, Lomborg argues, species may be constantly passing into extinction regardless of the carbon content of the atmosphere. "Since life on Earth began with the first bacteria 3.5 billion years ago, species getting blotted out has been part and parcel of evolution," Lomborg says. "Those species which could not survive became extinct. Extinction is the ultimate destiny of every living species."[71]

"Of the thirteen populations of polar bears in Canada, 11 are stable or increasing in number. . . . It is just silly to predict the demise of polar bears in 25 years based on [climate change] hysteria."[63]

— Mitchell Taylor, Canadian biologist.

Canada's Troubled Forests

Large forested areas can often help reduce the impact of greenhouse gases because plants absorb carbon dioxide. In recent years, though, studies have determined that Canada's 1.2 million square miles (3.1 square km) of forests do not do a good job of absorbing carbon.

Because of warmer temperatures, populations of pine bark beetles have attacked trees in Canada. About 50,000 acres of pine trees in British Columbia have been stricken by the pests. Experts can tell when the trees are under stress by the beetles—the pine needles turn red and fall to the ground. Said James Snetsinger, chief forester for British Columbia, "Once those infested trees are killed by the pine beetle, they are no longer sequestering carbon."

Warmer temperatures have also led to wildfires, which release carbon into the atmosphere. Moreover, scientists fear that Canada's logging industry churns up "forest peat," soil that includes the remains of old trees. The peat contains huge amounts of carbon absorbed by trees during their lifetimes. As loggers disturb the terrain, carbon can be stirred up and released into the atmosphere. The forest peat found in Canada's woodlands is estimated to store 186 billion tons (182 billion metric tons) of carbon.

Quoted in Howard Witt, "Canada's Forests, Once Huge Help on Greenhouse Gases, Now Contribute to Climate Change," *Chicago Tribune*, January 2, 2009. www.chicagotribune.com.

Saga of the Woolly Mammoth

Climate change skeptics point to the story of the woolly mammoth as an example of an animal that failed to adapt. The huge, elephant-like mammoth lived in North America but passed into extinction about 12,000 years ago. For years, scientists believed that the mammoths were killed off by human hunters, but new evidence has surfaced suggesting that other species that lived side by side with the mammoths—such as bison and elk—managed to survive even though they were hunted as often as mammoths.

Why did bison and elk survive, yet the mammoths died out? According to studies made by zoologist Dale Guthrie of the University of Alaska, the region of Alaska and the Yukon Territory in Canada underwent something of a climate change. Warmer temperatures enhanced the growth of grasses. The bison, elk, and mammoths flourished during this period.

Then, the climate changed again. Temperatures cooled. The tall grasses were replaced by forested areas. According to Guthrie, the bison and elk were able to adapt to the new food sources, but the mammoths did not, and the species eventually fell into extinction. "Humans were probably hunting some of the animals that went extinct, but 1,000 years after the humans came in [bison

Failure to adapt to a changing environment may explain the extinction of the woolly mammoth. The massive elephant-like creatures died out even as other animals of the same period, such as bison and elk, flourished.

and elk] were still doing fine,"[72] he says. Therefore, while changing temperatures did help to speed the extinction of the woolly mammoths, their demise resulted from their failure to adapt to their changing environment, not the presence of carbon in the atmosphere.

Lomborg adds that biology and zoology developed into modern sciences over the past 100 years or so. He wonders whether biologists and zoologists are constantly unearthing evidence of dying species simply because there are now more biologists and zoologists than there were a century ago.

If more scientists are looking for extinctions, then more scientists are also finding new species. In fact, Lomborg says, earth is constantly spawning new varieties of living things. According to statistics gathered by Lomborg, more than 80 million different species are currently living on the planet. "Never before have there been so many species as there are now,"[73] he says.

> "I don't think there is any question polar bears are in danger from global warming. People who deny that have a clear interest in hunting bears."[64]
>
> — Andrew Derocher, University of Alberta biologist.

Can Nature Cope?

Climate change skeptics often complain about the visual images used by the environmental community to call attention to climate change—often, photographs of polar bears clinging to ice floes. They disagree with such messages, suggesting that they do not tell the whole story. Indeed, scientists such as Taylor believe that more polar bears are alive now than two decades ago. Meanwhile, other skeptics do not deny that some species have disappeared—but the extinction of species is a scientific fact that predates the debate over climate change. Lomborg points out that millions of species have lived and died on earth since the first one-celled organisms formed on the planet more than 3 billion years ago.

Other scientists say the evidence of climate change on the environment cannot be ignored. They point to the deterioration of the coral reefs, the death of the pine and ash trees, the jellyfish attacks on the swimmers of the Mediterranean Sea, the spread of disease by mosquitoes and bats, and hundreds of other examples that illustrate how nature can no longer cope with a warming planet.

Facts

- Inuit guides can earn as much as $25,000 leading hunting parties in search of polar bears—a clear reason, critics suggest, that Inuit leaders insist the polar bears are not endangered by climate change.

- Scientists have found that the Pacific Ocean experienced a period of warmth during the Little Ice Age as well as cooler temperatures during the Medieval Warm Period, suggesting that coral has thrived independent of changes in the earth's climate.

- Biologist Kent Carpenter, who conducted a worldwide inventory of coral reefs, has predicted that all corals will fall into extinction within the next century.

- The U.S. Government Accountability Office has found evidence of environmental damage caused by climate change in national parks and other federally protected lands and waters that comprise about 30 percent of the United States.

- A study by the environmental groups World Conservation Union and Conservation International concludes that about one-third of the world's amphibian species are heading toward extinction.

- The University of Leeds in Great Britain has found that due to climate change, between 15 and 35 percent of land-dwelling plants and animals are in danger of disappearing by 2050.

- In 2004, four polar bears were found dead in the Beaufort Sea north of Alaska; scientists concluded the bears drowned because the polar ice cap had receded some 160 miles (258km), forcing them to swim longer distances.

How Has the World Responded to Climate Change?

A nation that has truly committed itself to reducing carbon emissions is Taiwan, particularly in the city of Kaohsiung. In 2005 the Taiwanese government unveiled plans to build a new sports stadium in Kaohsiung. Known as World Games Stadium, the facility seats more than 40,000 sports fans. Four years after plans for the stadium were announced, construction was completed and the stadium hosted its first sporting event, an Olympic-style track and field tournament. While the eyes of the spectators were glued on the athletes competing on the field, perhaps the most interesting feature of the stadium could be found overhead: The facility's 230,000-square-foot roof (21,368 square m) is almost completely covered with solar panels.

The panels make so much electricity that the stadium does not have to rely on power that would ordinarily be made through coal-fired energy plants. In fact, the solar panels make more electricity than the stadium uses. The excess power is fed into the local electricity grid, where it helps power many of the homes and businesses in Kaohsiung, a city of 1.5 million people. Said Liu Shyh-fang, managing director of the World Games 2009 Kaohsiung Organizing Committee, "The main stadium is the brightest World Games star."[74]

Certainly, Taiwan is not alone in supporting green energy initiatives. The American government, as well as many foreign governments, has taken some steps to reduce fossil fuel emissions. For example, the U.S. government has provided tax incentives for home owners and businesses to convert to solar power and other alternative energy sources that do not rely on fossil fuels and, therefore, emit no greenhouse gases. Some state governments have also provided tax incentives as well as cash awards to people and companies to help them convert to alternative energy. In 2009 the federal government provided rebates to the owners of gas-guzzling vehicles to trade them in for smaller, more fuel-efficient cars. Under the so-called "cash for clunkers" program nearly 700,000 gas guzzlers were taken off American roads.

Still, more than two decades after NASA scientist James E. Hansen first warned Congress about the approaching crisis of global warming, environmentalists say they are far from satisfied with the measures taken by the U.S. government to reduce or eliminate carbon emissions. They also believe the governments of many other industrialized nations have been slow to respond to the alarms raised by members of the scientific community. Says Andy Atkins, executive director of the environmental group Friends of the Earth, "The

Construction crews work on the solar-paneled roof of the World Games Stadium in Kaohsiung, Taiwan, in preparation for the 2009 athletic event. Excess electricity generated by the panels powers homes and businesses in this city of 1.5 million people.

developed world, which has done most to create this crisis, must face up to its global responsibilities. . . . Time is running out—we need bold action."[75]

The Kyoto Protocol

Two major international efforts to rein in fossil fuel emissions have been made within the past two decades. In 1997 nearly 200 countries sent representatives to Kyoto, Japan, to negotiate the terms of an international treaty designed to reduce carbon emissions 5 percent below 1990 levels. The United States took a lead role in negotiating the terms of the pact; Al Gore, at the time the vice president, headed the U.S. delegation in Japan.

After the so-called Kyoto Protocol was negotiated, though, two U.S. presidents—Bill Clinton and George W. Bush—refused to submit it to the U.S. Senate for ratification. Clinton and Bush both contended that the Kyoto Protocol would have a devastating impact on American industries, forcing them to cut back on production and, therefore, to reduce their workforces. With the world's most important industrial power—and, at the time, the most significant polluter—balking at ratifying the Kyoto Protocol, the pact was doomed to failure.

"The failure to [control] carbon leaves a giant hole in the U.S. energy and climate policy, and the long-term cost to the United States will be enormous." [81]

— Rafe Pomerance, president of the environmental group Clean Air Cool Planet.

The Copenhagen Accord

In late 2009 the nations of the world tried again. Some 200 countries sent delegates to a United Nations conference on climate change held in Copenhagen, Denmark. President Barack Obama as well as the leaders of some 100 countries took a personal hand in negotiating the agreement, which specifies that their countries would take steps to ensure that the average global temperature does not rise another 3.6°F (2°C) and that developed countries must cut their carbon emissions by 20 percent by 2020.

President Barack Obama acknowledged that in the past the United States and other industrialized nations had been slow to address climate change. He hoped the Copenhagen Accord would mark a new beginning. "We know the fault lines because we've been imprisoned by them for years," he said.

But here is the bottom line: we can embrace this accord, take a substantial step forward, and continue to refine it and build upon its foundation or we can again choose delay, falling back into the same divisions that have stood in the way of action for years. And we will be back having the same stale arguments month after month, year after year—all while the danger of climate change grows until it is irreversible.[76]

Still, even as Obama and other world leaders announced their agreement on the Copenhagen Accord, the pact came under fire from environmentalists who complained that it did not go far enough to rein in fossil fuel emissions. Scottish climate scientist David Reay said that a 20 percent cut in emissions would not be effective in slowing climate change and that world leaders would do well to double their goal. "If we are to be successful in preventing the worst impacts of climate change then world leaders from the industrialized nations must commit to reducing emissions by at least 40 per cent by 2020,"[77] Reay said.

Moreover, critics complained that the pact is not binding—no countries would suffer consequences if they ignored the terms of the deal. "The striking and hopeful thing about the speeches given by the leaders of the major carbon-emitting nations was the firmness with which almost all of them reiterated their unilateral commitment to making significant, if inadequate, cuts in emissions," said Carl Pope, president of the Sierra Club, a major American environmental group. "Not only the United States, Europe, China, and India but also virtually every other nation that is a significant source of emissions promised to act. Equally striking, but depressing, was their unwillingness or inability to transform these individual intentions into a robust collective response."[78]

Cap and Trade

Some of the world leaders who attended the Copenhagen conference conceded that the agreement had its shortcomings. "This is the first step we are taking towards a green and low-carbon future for the world, steps we are taking together," said Gordon Brown, at the time the prime minister of Great Britain, "but like all first

How Efficient Are Wind and Solar Energy?

Some experts suggest that renewable energy sources such as wind, solar, and geothermal power could never completely replace fossil fuels because they are largely inefficient. After all, they argue, the sun stops making energy at night and on cloudy or rainy days, solar panels produce little power. Meanwhile, wind turbines are only effective when the wind blows—on days of little breeze, the turbines produce little power.

In fact, during gale-force winds, many turbines have to be shut down because they are in danger of breaking apart. Jesse H. Ausubel, a senior research associate for the Rockefeller University in New York, points out that solar arrays and so-called "wind farms" typically take up hundreds of acres of ground, a lot of which is now in prime agricultural use. "Rapidly exhausted economies of scale stop wind," he argues. "One hundred windy square meters, a good size for a Manhattan apartment, can power a lamp or two, but not the clothes washer and dryer, microwave oven, plasma TVs or computers or dozens of other devices in the apartment, or the apartments above or below it. New York City would require every square meter of Connecticut to become a wind farm."

Jesse H. Ausubel, "Renewable and Nuclear Heresies," *International Journal of Nuclear Governance, Economy and Ecology*, November 3, 2007.

steps, the steps are difficult and they are hard. I know what we really need is a legally binding treaty as quickly as possible."[79]

As the delegates returned home to sell the Copenhagen Accord to their own governments, it became clear why a much stronger and binding agreement had eluded them. At home, they faced hostility from concerned political and industry leaders who believe that reducing carbon emissions would cost jobs and slow economic growth. In America and elsewhere, the effort to reduce carbon emissions was concentrated on a so-called "cap and trade" policy that would enable large industrial polluters to buy credits, also known as offsets, to emit carbon from their smokestacks. The sellers of the offsets are industries that have found ways to cap emissions. It is believed that a robust market in the carbon credits will emerge, prompting many large companies to cut their carbon emissions dramatically so that they will be able to earn substantial profits by selling the offsets to polluters who cannot find ways to scale back on carbon emissions.

In 2009 the U.S. House adopted a cap and trade bill drafted by Representatives Henry Waxman of California and Edward J. Markey of Massachusetts. The goal of the Waxman-Markey bill was to cut carbon emissions to a level that is 4 percent lower than the level of emissions produced in 1990. Although the House passed Waxman-Markey, the bill died in the Senate. Many opponents of the measure feared the legislation could cost jobs by making it more expensive for carbon-emitting industries to manufacture goods. A typical complaint was voiced by Senator Carte Goodwin of West Virginia. His state is home to a significant coal mining industry, which could be hurt if electrical utilities cut back on their use of coal. Said Goodwin, "With regard to cap and trade, I will say this: From what I've seen of the Waxman-Markey bill that passed the House of Representatives and other proposals pending in the Senate, they simply are not right for West Virginia. . . . I will not support any piece of legislation that threatens any West Virginia job, any West Virginia family, or jeopardizes the long-term economic security of this state."[80]

Environmentalists were stunned by the failure of the Senate to adopt a cap and trade law. Said Rafe Pomerance, president of the environmental group Clean Air Cool Planet, "As the Earth's climate continues to rapidly move into unchartered territory, the U.S. Senate needs to act. The failure to [control] carbon leaves a giant hole in the U.S. energy and climate policy, and the long-term cost to the United States will be enormous."[81]

An Influential Minority

One of the reasons for the death of cap and trade in the Senate was that an influential minority of senators has never accepted the

> "Thus far no one has seriously demonstrated any scientific proof that increased global temperatures would lead to the catastrophes predicted by alarmists."[82]
>
> — U.S. senator James Inhofe of Oklahoma.

science behind climate change. (Unlike the House, where legislation can pass with a simple majority vote, the Senate requires 60 votes to adopt legislation—therefore, 41 senators can effectively kill legislation.) "It's . . . important to question whether global warming is even a problem for human existence," insists U.S. senator James Inhofe of Oklahoma. "Thus far no one has seriously demonstrated any scientific proof that increased global temperatures would lead to the catastrophes predicted by alarmists. In fact, it appears that just the opposite is true: that increases in global temperatures may have a beneficial effect on how we live our lives."[82]

Moreover, some members of Congress have not only been hesitant to adopt laws that would rein in fossil fuel emissions but believe the American government should be doing more to help energy companies find new reserves of oil, coal, and natural gas. Indeed, the petroleum industry has called for Congress to open up new areas of the country for oil and gas exploration—specifically a vast, 19-million-acre territory (7.7 million ha) in Alaska known as the Arctic National Wildlife Refuge (ANWR). In addition, in 2010 oil companies sought permission to establish new offshore drilling platforms in the Chukchi Sea, which is off the coast of northwest Alaska. Conservationists oppose drilling in the sea, which they believe is environmentally sensitive.

> "Instead of drilling for more dirty oil, we can shift to clean energy that will create jobs, combat global warming, and keep our wildlife and wild places intact."[86]
>
> — Dan Ritzman, Alaska program director for the Sierra Club.

Vast Oil Reserves

According to the U.S. Geological Survey, reserves of more than 100 billion barrels of oil may be available in the ANWR, the Chukchi Sea, and other portions of North America near or above the Arctic Circle. Said a report by the Geological Survey, "Most of the Arctic, especially offshore, is essentially unexplored with respect to petroleum. The extensive Arctic continental shelves may constitute the geographically largest unexplored prospective area for petroleum remaining on Earth."[83]

The oil industry contends that those reserves could make Americans less dependent on oil imported from the Middle East and other foreign lands. Indeed, even some environmentalists acknowledge that energy security should be an issue of major concern to Americans—certainly as important to Americans as climate change. Says Sascha Müller-Kraenner, an author and policy adviser to the environmental group Nature Conservancy, "A reliable energy supply is one of the basic prerequisites for a functioning economy."[84] In fact, the American Petroleum Institute believes the availability of such oil reserves would enhance the growth of American industry, helping to create more than 160,000 American jobs. One advocate for drilling in the ANWR is U.S. senator Lisa Murkowski of Alaska, who says, "What ANWR represents to this country is energy security and national security."[85]

Many environmentalists counter that finding access to more than 100 billion barrels of oil in the Arctic will not enhance the nation's security—not when rising global temperatures are ruining crops, wiping out species, and spreading disease. Says Dan Ritzman, Alaska program director for the Sierra Club, "Instead of drilling for more dirty oil, we can shift to clean energy that will create jobs, combat global warming, and keep our wildlife and wild places intact."[86]

Alaska's Arctic National Wildlife Refuge (pictured), valued for its pristine wilderness areas, may have further value as a huge source of oil. Opening the wildlife refuge to oil exploration is a source of fervid debate in Congress and among environmentalists and the energy industry.

Wrong Strategy

Other world leaders who returned to their homes from Copenhagen anxious to implement carbon-controlling measures found similar hostilities in their countries as well. Among those countries were Japan, France, Canada, and Australia, where leaders found lawmakers also concerned about the loss of jobs. In Australia, legislators had approved a very ambitious cap and trade system. At first, the system included just modest goals, cutting carbon emissions 5 percent below 2000 levels.

Eventually, though, Australia's plan would become much more significant, cutting carbon emissions to a level 25 percent below 1990 levels and, by 2020, to a level 40 percent below 1990 levels. But as the country sank into an economic recession, lawmakers agreed to postpone even the modest start of the program to 2011. "The worst global recession since the Great Depression means we must adapt our climate change measures but not abandon them," said Australian prime minister Kevin Rudd. "Our objective, of course, is to provide business certainty for the future."[87]

Other critics suggested that cap and trade is simply the wrong strategy. Lomborg suggests that the way to rein in carbon emissions is not to make it more expensive to burn oil and coal, which would occur under cap and trade, but to make it cheaper for energy consumers to convert to solar, wind, and other alternative energy sources. He says national governments would do well to offer a wide array of economic incentives such as tax breaks and grants to help homeowners and businesses convert. By offering economic incentives to convert, Lomborg argues, businesses and individuals would, on their own, reduce their reliance on fossil fuels. "Such a commitment would resolve many of today's political challenges," Lomborg insists. "Developing nations would be much more likely to embrace a positive path of innovation than a punitive one that handicaps their abilities to grow their economies."[88]

Small Steps

While it would seem as though countries are hesitant to take giant steps such as enacting sweeping cap and trade policies, many have been willing to enact lesser measures. In addition to the cash for clunkers program, many American homeowners were able to

The World's Top Polluters

China, which has been undergoing rapid industrialization in recent years, overtook the United States in 2007 as the world's top emitter of greenhouse gases. According to the Union of Concerned Scientists, China energy users emit 6.6 billion tons (6 billion metric tons) of carbon dioxide a year. Energy users in the United States emit 6.5 billion tons (5.9 billion metric tons) of carbon dioxide a year.

Other top carbon producers are Russia, 1.8 billion tons (1.7 billion metric tons); India, 1.42 billion tons (1.29 billion metric tons); Japan, 1.36 billion tons (1.24 billion metric tons); Germany, 944 million tons (857 million metric tons); Canada, 676 million tons (614 million metric tons); Great Britain, 644 million tons (585 million metric tons); South Korea, 566 million tons (514 million metric tons); and Iran, 519 million tons (471 million metric tons).

"This is the best and most up to date estimate available," said Joseph Olivier, senior scientist for the Netherlands Environmental Assessment Agency, which tracks worldwide fossil fuel emissions. "China relies very heavily on coal and all of the recent trends show their emissions going up very quickly."

John Vidal and David Adam, "China Overtakes U.S. as World's Biggest CO2 Emitter," *London Guardian*, June 19, 2007. www.guardian.co.uk.

take advantage of a similar rebate program in 2010, offering them financial incentives to replace old washers, dryers, refrigerators, and similar energy-wasting heavy appliances for newer, energy-efficient models. Congress has also made tax cuts available to the buyers of electric cars, which started rolling off the production lines in 2010. The tax breaks shave $7,500 off the prices of those cars.

In addition, in 2007 Congress adopted new efficiency standards for light bulbs that will essentially outlaw incandescent bulbs by 2014. By then, most Americans will instead be using compact fluorescent light (CFL) bulbs, which use 75 percent less electricity and last 10 times longer than incandescent bulbs—meaning it takes far less fossil fuel to illuminate CFLs than it takes to make incandescent bulbs light up.

Going Beyond Congress

Some state governments have gone beyond what Congress has enacted and instituted their own laws designed to reduce carbon emissions. Other states have been slow to act, though, out of fear that if they start mandating changes in energy use they would place constraints on businesses and, therefore, slow economic expansion. Still, in 2010 the advocacy group Environment America reported that efforts underway in several states would result in a cut in carbon emissions of some 7 percent by 2020—certainly, not enough to meet the terms of the Copenhagen Accord but, nevertheless, a sign of progress.

One state that has taken positive steps is California, which established a goal of reducing carbon emissions within its borders by 25 percent by 2020. In California, lawmakers have mandated new energy-efficiency standards for television sets, which now account for as much as 10 percent of the average household's energy use. The new efficiency rules for TV sets are estimated to save California consumers $1 billion a year in energy bills while removing some 3 million tons of carbon from the atmosphere. Environment America's California chapter said in a statement, "It is small steps like these that will take California to its overall goal."[89]

Other states have found less success. In Pennsylvania, for example, lawmakers have been able to adopt modest measures designed to reduce dependence on fossil fuels, but stricter measures have been stalled by fierce opposition. In 2004 the Pennsylvania General Assembly passed a law requiring electrical utilities in the state to make 0.5 percent of their electricity from renewable resources, such as solar and wind power. With the renewable energy bar set so low, all of the state's power companies found it easy to meet the letter of the law.

In 2010 state lawmakers revisited the issue and proposed an increase in the requirement to 3 percent. Under the terms of the legislation, lawmakers proposed to give electric companies plenty of time to ramp up—they decided that the 3 percent goal would not have to be met until 2024.

Like West Virginia, Pennsylvania is home to a substantial coal mining industry. Officials from the industry reacted bitterly to the renewable energy proposal and instructed their lobbyists in the state capital of Harrisburg to pressure lawmakers to kill the legislation. The coal industry lobbyists contended that if electrical utilities made more of their energy through solar and wind power, they would buy less coal, which would put coal miners out of work. Not wanting to put people out of work amid a national economic recession, state legislators in Pennsylvania agreed to kill the bill. Indeed, when reporters advised the coal industry's chief lobbyist, Pennsylvania Coal Association president George Ellis, that it appeared as though the renewable energy law was likely to be killed, he responded, "That's great."[90]

Searching for the Answers

The efforts made by government leaders in places like Australia, Kyoto, and Copenhagen illustrate how difficult addressing climate change can be. For every leap forward taken in a place such as Kaohsiung, an effort is stalled in a place such as Pennsylvania. Certainly, many government leaders understand they do have a responsibility to protect the environment of earth, but they are also pressed by economic concerns. No politician wants to cast votes that would put his or her constituents out of work. The fact that climate scientists have yet to convince Inhofe, Murkowski, and other American lawmakers of the need to rein in fossil fuel emissions suggests that work still needs to be done to enhance the evidence supporting their claims.

In the meantime, the debate over the greenhouse effect is sure to rage on as earth's temperature continues to rise. Whether that rise in temperature is due to the human activity of burning fossil fuels or through a natural heating cycle that has been ongoing for many years is an issue that a lot of people believe has yet to be answered. And so, as people leave their homes in places like Shishmaref, as the coral turns white and crumbly along the Great Barrier Reef, as polar bears head north for refuge, politicians in Washington, D.C., and other world capitals will continue to search for the answers to why this is happening.

> "The worst global recession since the Great Depression means we must adapt our climate change measures but not abandon them. Our objective, of course, is to provide business certainty for the future."[87]
>
> — Australian prime minister Kevin Rudd.

Facts

- The roof of World Games Stadium in Kaohsiung, Taiwan, holds 4,482 solar panels; the panels eliminate 660 tons of carbon dioxide that would otherwise be emitted into the atmosphere each year.

- Twenty-nine states require electric companies operating within their borders to make some percentage of their energy through renewable resources such as solar or wind power. Among the leaders is Rhode Island, which has mandated that by 2020, 16 percent of the state's energy must come from alternative resources.

- The U.S. Congress has mandated that new cars and trucks must average at least 35.5 miles per gallon of gasoline by 2012, a standard that would cut greenhouse gas emissions by 40 percent over fuel efficiency regulations in effect in 2009.

- To help scrub the atmosphere of carbon, China has announced its intentions to plant new forests on 20 percent of the country's land mass—an area comprising some 740,000 square miles.

- Each year, in late March, the World Wildlife Fund sponsors "Earth Hour" to call attention to climate change. To participate, millions of people shut off lights and electrical appliances for one hour. In recent years, participants have included operators of the Sydney Opera House in Australia; hotels along the Las Vegas strip; the Colosseum in Rome, Italy; and the Eiffel Tower in Paris, France.

- In 2010 the New York City Council adopted a measure requiring the city's 22,000 largest residential and commercial buildings, which are believed to be responsible for half the city's carbon emissions, to undergo periodic energy audits. It is believed that the audits will help reduce carbon emissions in the city 30 percent by 2030.

Related Organizations and Web Sites

American Petroleum Institute (API)

1220 L St. NW
Washington, DC 20005
phone: (202) 682-8000
Web site: www.api.org

The API is a trade organization representing oil and gas companies. Visitors to its site can download the reports *Climate Challenge: A Progress Report* and *Companies Address Climate Change*. The reports explain how the API and oil companies are working to develop better carbon detection methods and reduce carbon emissions from their fuels.

Center for Global Change and Arctic System Research

University of Alaska
930 Koyukuk Dr., Room 306 IARC
Fairbanks, AK 99775
phone: (907) 474-5818
fax: (907) 474-6722
e-mail: cgc@iarc.uaf.edu
Web site: www.cgc.uaf.edu

The center monitors how climate change has affected the environment of the Arctic region. Visitors to the center's Web site can download copies of *Impacts of a Warming Arctic*, which illustrates how temperatures have risen in the Arctic, how ice in the region has receded, and how wildlife is affected by the warming temperatures.

Institute for Energy Research

1415 S. Voss Rd., Suite 110-287
Houston, TX 77057
phone: (713) 974-1918
fax: (713) 974-1993
Web site: http://instituteforenergyresearch.org

The institute argues that climate change is not as serious as environmentalists suggest and that restricting fossil fuel use could lead to economic disaster. Available on its Web site are the institute's positions on cap and trade, government-mandated emissions caps, warming and cooling trends, and the accuracy of climate science.

Intergovernmental Panel on Climate Change

World Meteorological Organization
7bis Avenue de la Paix
C.P. 2300
CH-1211
Geneva 2, Switzerland
phone: 41 22 730 8208 / 54 / 84
fax: 41 22 730 8025 / 13
e-mail: IPCC-SEC@wmo.int
Web site: www.ipcc.ch

The panel, an international organization that monitors global warming, won the Nobel Peace Prize for its work in focusing attention on global warming. The panel's periodic reports detailing the threats of climate change can be accessed through the organization's Web site.

International Energy Agency (IEA)

9 Rue de la Fédération
75739 Paris Cedex 15, France
phone: 33 1 40 57 65 00/01
fax: 33 1 40 57 65 09
e-mail: ghginfo@iea.org
Web site: www.iea.org

The IEA monitors energy use throughout the world. The link to "Statistics" on its Web site shows the amounts of oil, coal, natural gas, and other forms of energy consumed by every country on earth. The agency also maintains an online archive of numerous news stories about energy consumption and how fossil fuel use affects climate change.

National Aeronautics and Space Administration (NASA)

Jet Propulsion Laboratory, California Institute of Technology
4800 Oak Grove Dr.
Pasadena, CA 91109
phone: (818) 354-4321
Web site: http://climate.nasa.gov

NASA provides satellite images and other resources to climatologists. It maintains a Web site that shows ongoing monitors of sea level, global temperatures, polar ice, and carbon dioxide. By accessing the link to "Images of Change," students can view satellite photos showing how the earth's terrain has been affected by global warming.

Scripps Institute of Oceanography

University of California at San Diego
9500 Gilman Dr.
La Jolla, CA 92093
phone: (858) 534-3624
e-mail: scrippsnews@ucsd.edu
Web site: http://sio.ucsd.edu

The institute researches many topics related to global warming, particularly how climate change affects marine life. By accessing the link to "Research Highlights" on the institute's Web site, students can learn about how warmer oceans have affected fish life and how climate change often affects drinking water supplies.

Stop Global Warming

15332 Antioch St., Suite 168
Pacific Palisades, CA 90272
phone: (310) 454-5726
Web site: www.stopglobalwarming.org

The group promotes efforts to reduce greenhouse gas emissions. Visitors to the group's Web site can find information on many energy-saving techniques, such as using compact fluorescent bulbs and recycled paper, running the dishwasher when it is full, installing low-flow showerheads, and buying farm products that are grown locally.

United Nations Framework Convention on Climate Change

Haus Carstanjen, Martin-Luther-King-Strasse 8
53175 Bonn, Germany

phone: 49 228 815 1000
fax: 49 228 815 1999
e-mail: secretariat@unfccc.int
Web site: http://unfccc.int

This organization was established by the United Nations to oversee the Copenhagen Accords, the agreement reached by 200 nations to reduce greenhouse gas emissions. By visiting the organization's Web site, students can read the terms of the accord as well as updates on the actions taken by countries to cut carbon emissions by 20 percent by 2020.

U.S. Department of Energy (DOE)
1000 Independence Ave. SW
Washington, DC 20585
phone: (202) 586-5000
fax: (202) 586-4403
e-mail: The.Secretary@hq.doe.gov
Web site: www.energy.gov

The department monitors energy use in the United States. Its site offers resources about greenhouse gas emissions and a link to the U.S. Climate Change Technology Program, where students can read about the development of new technologies designed to help reduce fossil fuel emissions and enhance the effectiveness of renewable resources.

U.S. Environmental Protection Agency (EPA)
Ariel Rios Bldg.
1200 Pennsylvania Ave. NW
Washington, DC 20460
phone: (202) 272-0167
Web site: www.epa.gov

The EPA is the federal government's chief watchdog over the environment, responsible for monitoring carbon emissions. Students who visit the EPA's Web site can use the Household Emissions Calculator to determine how much carbon their families are emitting into the atmosphere through household energy use.

Additional Reading

Books

Al Gore, *Our Choice: A Plan to Solve the Climate Crisis*. Emmaus, PA: Rodale, 2009.

Christopher Horner, *Red Hot Lies: How Global Warming Alarmists Use Threats, Fraud and Deception to Keep You Misinformed*. Washington, DC: Regnery, 2008.

Ian Plimer, *Heaven and Earth: Global Warming—the Missing Science*. Victoria, Australia: Connor Court, 2009.

Gavin Schmidt and Joshua Wolfe, *Climate Change: Picturing the Scene*. New York: W.W. Norton, 2009.

Linda Starke, ed., *State of the World 2009: Into a Warming World*. New York: W.W. Norton, 2009.

Periodicals

James Delingpole, "Meet the Man Who Has Exposed the Great Climate Change Con Trick," *Spectator*, July 11, 2009.

Juliet Eilperin and David A. Fahrenthold, "Series of Missteps by Climate Scientists Threatens Climate Change Agenda," *Washington Post*, February 15, 2010.

David A. Fahrenthold, "Scientists' Use of Computer Models to Predict Climate Change Is Under Attack," *Washington Post*, April 6, 2010.

Andrew C. Revken, "Industry Ignored Its Scientists on Climate," *New York Times*, April 24, 2009.

Bryan Walsh, "A River Ran Through It," *Time*, December 14, 2009.

Internet Sources

Earth Observatory, "The Keeling Curve." http://earthobservatory.nasa.gov/IOTD/view.php?id=5620.

Al Gore, "Nobel Peace Prize Lecture," December 10, 2007. http://nobelprize.org/nobel_prizes/peace/laureates/2007/gore-lecture_en.html.

James Inhofe, "The Science of Climate Change," U.S. Senate Floor Speech, July 28, 2003. http://inhofe.senate.gov/pressreleases/climate.htm.

U.S. Global Change Research Program, *Global Climate Change Impacts in the United States*. www.globalchange.gov/publications/reports/scientific-assessments/us-impacts.

World Health Organization, *Protecting Health from Climate Change*. www.who.int/globalchange/publications/reports/9789241598880/en/index.html.

Source Notes

Introduction: The Vanishing Village

1. Quoted in John D. Sutter, "Climate Change Threatens Life in Shishmaref, Alaska," CNN, December 3, 2009. www.cnn.com.

2. Quoted in David Willis, "Sea Engulfing Alaskan Village," BBC, July 30, 2004. http://news.bbc.co.uk.

3. Edmund Contoski, "Global Warming, Global Myth," *Liberty*, September 2008. www.libertyunbound.com.

4. Peter C. Glover, "Media Credibility, Not Ice Caps, In Meltdown," *American Thinker*, February 23, 2009. www.american thinker.com.

5. Quoted in Sutter, "Climate Change Threatens Life in Shishmaref, Alaska."

Chapter One: What Are the Origins of the Climate Change Controversy?

6. Quoted in Andrew C. Revkin, "Special Report: Endless Summer—Living with the Greenhouse Effect," *Discover*, October 1988. http://discovermagazine.com.

7. S. Fred Singer, "Fact and Fancy on Greenhouse Earth," *Wall Street Journal*, August 30, 1988, p. 22.

8. Henry Ford and Ray Leone Faurote, *My Philosophy of Industry*. New York: Coward-McCann, 1929, p. 56.

9. Quoted in David Malakoff, "Revisiting the 'Keeling Curve,'" National Public Radio, January 28, 2009. www.npr.org.

10. Spencer R. Weart, *The Discovery of Global Warming*. Cambridge, MA: Harvard University Press, 2003, p. 38.

11. Al Gore, "Nobel Peace Prize Lecture," December 10, 2007. http://nobelprize.org.

12. Singer, "Fact and Fancy on Greenhouse Earth," p. 22.

13. Bjørn Lomborg, "The State of the World," *Skeptic*, 2002, p. 62.

14. Quoted in Michael J. McCarthy, "Is the Crazy Weather Still Another Sign of Climate Shift?" *Wall Street Journal*, August 18, 1988, p. 1.

15. Quoted in William K. Stevens, "Scientists Link '88 Drought to Natural Cycle in Tropical Pacific," *New York Times*, January 3, 1989, p. C-1.

16. Quoted in Will Stewart, "Russia's Top Weatherman's Blow to Climate Change Lobby as He Says Winter in Siberia May Be Coldest on Record," *London Daily Mail*, March 24, 2010. www.dailymail.co.uk.

17. Quoted in Stewart, "Russia's Top Weatherman's Blow to Climate Change Lobby."

18. Quoted in Media Matters, "Brain Freeze: Conservative Media Still Using Winter Weather to Attack Global Warming," February 9, 2010. http://mediamatters.org.

19. Quoted in Media Matters, "Brain Freeze."

20. Rob Gutro, "What's the Difference Between Weather and Climate?" National Aeronautics and Space Administration Science News Team, February 1, 2005. www.nasa.gov.

Chapter Two: How Reliable Is the Science of Climate Change?

21. Quoted in Bryan Walsh, "A River Ran Through It," *Time*, December 14, 2009, p. 59.

22. Quoted in Walsh, "A River Ran Through It," p. 58.

23. Quoted in Walsh, "A River Ran Through It," p. 63.

24. Quoted in James Delingpole, "Meet the Man Who Has Exposed the Great Climate Change Con Trick," *Spectator*, July 11, 2009, p. 14.

25. Al Gore, "Hockey Stick," September 16, 2008. http://blog.algore.com/2008/09/hockey_stick.html.

26. David R. Legates, "Revising 1,000 Years of Climate History," National Center for Policy Analysis, August 8, 2003. www.ncpa.org.

27. Legates, "Revising 1,000 Years of Climate History."

28. Quoted in BBC, "Climate Legacy of 'Hockey Stick,'" August 16, 2004. http://news.bbc.co.uk.

29. Patrick J. Michaels, *Meltdown: The Predictable Distortion of Global Warming by Scientists*. Washington, DC: Cato Institute, 2004, p. 227.

30. Quoted in Juliet Eilperin and David A. Fahrenthold, "Series of Missteps by Climate Scientists Threatens Climate Change Agenda," *Washington Post*, February 15, 2010, p. A-1.

31. Quoted in Faye Flam, "Penn State Panel Fully Clears Climatologist," *Philadelphia Inquirer*, July 2, 2010, p. A-4.

32. Quoted in Flam, "Penn State Panel Fully Clears Climatologist."

33. Quoted in David A. Fahrenthold, "Scientists' Use of Computer Models to Predict Climate Change Is Under Attack," *Washington Post*, April 6, 2010, p. HE-1.

34. Quoted in Fahrenthold, "Scientists' Use of Computer Models to Predict Climate Change Is Under Attack."

35. Quoted in Richard A. Kerr, "Global Warming: Rising Global Temperature, Rising Uncertainty," *Science*, April 13, 2001, p. 192.

36. Quoted in Fahrenthold, "Scientists' Use of Computer Models to Predict Climate Change Is Under Attack."

37. Quoted in Kerr, "Global Warming: Rising Global Temperature, Rising Uncertainty," p. 192.

38. Quoted in Andrew C. Revken, "Industry Ignored Its Scientists on Climate," *New York Times*, April 24, 2009, A-1.

39. Quoted in Revken, "Industry Ignored Its Scientists on Climate."

40. Quoted in Revken, "Industry Ignored Its Scientists on Climate."

41. Quoted in Revken, "Industry Ignored Its Scientists on Climate."

42. Quoted in Jeff Nesmith, "Foes of Global Warming Theory Have Energy Ties," Cox News Service, *Seattle Post-Intelligencer*, June 2, 2003. www.seattlepi.com.

Chapter Three: What Are the Potential Economic Impacts of Climate Change?

43. Quoted in Elizabeth Kolbert, "The Climate of Man—III," *New Yorker*, May 9, 2005, p. 52.

44. Quoted in Kolbert, "The Climate of Man—III," p. 54.

45. Edward Cameron, "Small Island Developing States at the Forefront of Global Climate Change," in Linda Starke, ed., *State of the World 2009: Into a Warming World*. New York: W.W. Norton, 2009, p. 71.

46. Quoted in *Global Times*, "Quest for Profit Overwhelms Defenses Against Flooding," August 3, 2010. http://opinion.globaltimes.cn.

47. Quoted in Mark Hertsgaard, "What Climate Change Means for Wine Industry," *Wired*, April 26, 2010. www.wired.com.

48. Quoted in Lauren Morello, "U.S. Study Projects How 'Unequivocal Warming' Will Change Americans' Lives," *New York Times*, June 17, 2009. www.nytimes.com.

49. Quoted in Catherine Rampell, "The Economic Impact of Climate Change," *New York Times*, June 16, 2009. http://economix.blogs.nytimes.com.

50. Quoted in David A. Fahrenthold, "Report on Warming Offers New Details," *Washington Post*, June 17, 2009. www.washington post.com.

51. Warren Meyer, "Warm Weather and Prosperity," July 27, 2009. www.climate-skeptic.com.

52. Quoted in Joel Achenbach, "The Tempest," *Washington Post*, May 28, 2006. www.washingtonpost.com.

53. William Gray, "We Are Not in a Climate Crisis," January 30, 2010. http://rayharvey.org.

54. Sallie Baliunas, "Warming Up to the Truth: The Real Story About Climate Change," Heritage Foundation, August 22, 2002. www.heritage.org.

55. American Petroleum Institute, "Put America to Work," June 15, 2010. www.api.org.

56. James D. Hamilton, "Oil Prices and the Economic Recession of 2007–2008," *VOX*, June 16, 2009. http://voxeu.org.

57. Quoted in John Dickerson, "What in the Hell Do They Think Is Causing It?" *Slate*, December 8, 2009. www.slate.com.

58. Al Gore, *Our Choice: A Plan to Solve the Climate Crisis*. Emmaus, PA: Rodale, 2009, p. 58.

Chapter Four: What Are the Potential Environmental Impacts of Climate Change?

59. Quoted in David Adam, "How Global Warming Sealed the Fate of the World's Coral Reefs," *Guardian*, September 2, 2009. www.guardian.co.uk.

60. Ian Plimer, *Heaven and Earth: Global Warming—the Missing Science*. Victoria, Australia: Connor Court, 2009, p. 318.

61. Gavin Schmidt and Joshua Wolfe, *Climate Change: Picturing the Scene*. New York: W.W. Norton, 2009, p. 130.

62. Quoted in Daniel Glick, "On Thin Ice," *National Wildlife*, December 1, 2006. www.nwf.org.

63. Quoted in U.S. Senate Committee on Environment and Public Works, "U.S. Senate Report Debunks Polar Bear Extinction Fears," January 30, 2008. http://epw.senate.gov.

64. Quoted in Fred Langan and Tom Leonard, "Polar Bears 'Thriving as Arctic Warms Up,'" *London Telegraph*, March 9, 2007. www.telegraph.co.uk.

65. Quoted in Brian Handwerk, "Frog Extinctions Linked to Global Warming," *National Geographic*, January 12, 2006. http://news.nationalgeographic.com.

66. Schmidt and Wolfe, *Climate Change: Picturing the Scene*, p. 120.

67. Quoted in *Brisbane Times*, "Hendra Virus Risk Rises as Bats Move South," August 17, 2009. www.brisbanetimes.com.au.

68. Schmidt and Wolfe, *Climate Change: Picturing the Scene*, p. 130.

69. Quoted in Monica Davey, "Balmy Weather May Bench a Baseball Staple," *New York Times*, July 11, 2007. www.nytimes.com.

70. Quoted in Don Hopey, "Tiny Bug May End Ash's Long Hitting Streak," *Pittsburgh Post-Gazette*, July 15, 2007. www.post-gazette.com.

71. Bjørn Lomborg, *The Skeptical Environmentalist: Measuring the Real State of the World*. Cambridge: Cambridge University Press, 2001, p. 249.

72. Quoted in Bjørn Carey, "Ancient Die-Off Blamed on Climate, Not Humans," MSNBC, May 10, 2006. www.msnbc.msn.com.

73. Lomborg, *The Skeptical Environmentalist*, p. 249.

Chapter Five: How Has the World Responded to Climate Change?

74. Quoted in Pat Gao, "The Games Go On," *Taiwan Review*, July 1, 2009. http://taiwanreview.nat.gov.tw.

75. Quoted in Friends of the Earth, "Brokenhagen—Climate Summit Ends in Failure," news release, December 19, 2009. www.foe.co.uk.

76. Quoted in Suzanne Goldenberg and Allegra Stratton, "Barack Obama's Speech Disappoints and Fuels Frustration in Copenhagen," *London Guardian*, December 18, 2009. www.guardian.co.uk.

77. Quoted in GAIA Discovery, "Top Climate Scientists Set 40 Percent Reduction of Carbon Emissions by 2020 for UN Climate Summit in Copenhagen," September 18, 2009. www.gaiadiscovery.com.

78. Carl Pope, "Lessons from Denmark," Huffington Post, December 21, 2009. www.huffingtonpost.com.

79. Quoted in John Vidal and Jonathan Watts, "Copenhagen Closes with Weak Deal That Poor Threaten to Reject," *London Guardian*, December 19, 2009. www.guardian.co.uk.

80. Quoted in Alex Kaplun, "New West Virginia Senator Signals Opposition to Cap and Trade," *New York Times*, July 16, 2010. www.nytimes.com.

81. Quoted in Renee Schoof, "Energy Bill Loses Steam in the Senate," *Philadelphia Inquirer*, July 23, 2010, p. A-13.

82. James Inhofe, "The Science of Climate Change," U.S. Senate Floor Speech, July 28, 2003. http://inhofe.senate.gov.

83. Quoted in CBC, "Equivalent of 112 Billion Barrels of Oil in North America's Arctic: Study," July 24, 2008. www.cbc.ca.

84. Sascha Müller-Kraenner, *Energy Security: Re-Measuring the World*. London: Earthscan, 2007, p. 21.

85. Quoted in Zachary Coile, "Senate Blocks Oil Drilling Push for Arctic Refuge," *San Francisco Chronicle*, December 22, 2005. www.sfgate.com.

86. Quoted in Wilderness Society, "Arctic Drilling Plan Gets Green Light; Analysis of Impacts Sorely Lacking," December 8, 2009. http://wilderness.org.

87. Quoted in *Telegraph*, "Australia's Carbon Emissions Trading Scheme Falls Victim to Recession," May 4, 2009. www.telegraph.co.uk.

88. Bjørn Lomborg, "Beyond Copenhagen," *Time*, December 14, 2009, p. 64.

89. Environment California, "Where the Action Is on Climate," January 3, 2010. www.environmentcalifornia.org.

90. Quoted in Diane Mastrull, "Backers Pessimistic over Pennsylvania Alt-Energy Bill," *Philadelphia Inquirer*, June 29, 2010. www.philly.com.

Index

Note: Page numbers in boldface
  indicate illustrations.

agriculture/food production, 59
  impacts of climate change on, 43,
    52
  warming as beneficial to, 44
American Petroleum Institute (API),
    37, 48, 79
Arctic
  impact of climate change in,
    55–56
  new passages opening in, 52
  oil reserves in, 72
Arctic National Wildlife Refuge
  (ANWR), 72, 73, **73**
Arrhenius, Svante, 15, 16
ash trees, threat to, 60–61
Atkins, Andy, 67
Ausubel, Jesse H., 70

Baliunas, Sallie, 46, 47
Barnett, Tim, 20
bears, 59
  polar, 55–56, 64, 65
Beluga Shipping, 52
Bernstein, Leonard S., 36
Bonaparte, Napoleon, 32
Bradley, Ray, 27, 28
Brown, Gordon, 69–70
Bush, George W., 68

California
  energy-efficiency standards set by,
    76
  grape industry, threats to, 42–43
Callendar, Guy Stewart, 34
Cameron, Edward, 41, 42
cap and trade, 69–71
  resistance to, 71–72, 74

carbon dioxide, 11
  atmospheric, first measurement of,
    15–17
  nations leading in emissions of, 75
  as percentage of total greenhouse
    gases, 17
Carboniferous Period, 23
Carpenter, Kent, 57, 65
cash-for-clunkers program, 67
Center for Global Change and Arctic
  System Research, 8, 79
China
  carbon dioxide emissions in, 75
  changes in weather patterns in,
    41–42
  reforestation efforts in, 78
climate, weather versus, 21–22
climate change
  cause of, 7, 15–17
  economic effects of, 41–43
  emission reductions required to
    prevent, 69
  extinctions caused by, 57–58
  refugees from, 49
  species displaced by, 58–59
  spread of disease associated with,
    59
Clinton, Bill, 68
coal, 47
coastal erosion, Alaskan villages
  threatened by, 9
compact fluorescent light (CFL)
  bulbs, 75–76
computer models, 31–33
  criticism of, 32–34
Conservation International, 65
Contoski, Edmund, 8
Copenhagen Accord (2009), 68–69,
  70
coral reefs, 53–55, **54**

bleaching of, 57
possible extinction of, 65
crude oil
    barrel of
        amount of gasoline produced
            by, 47
        size/products of, 23
    reserves of, 72–73
Curry, Judith, 27

Department of Energy, U.S. (DOE),
    17, 47, 51, 82
disease, climate change and spread
    of, 59
Doocy, Steve, 22
Downing, Thomas, 49
Drake, Edwin, 13

Earth Hour, 78
economy/economic impacts, 51, 52
    of inaction on global warming,
        41–44
    role of oil/gas in, 48–50
    of sudden cutback of fossil fuel
        use, 46–47
Ellis, George, 77
El Niño, 20
emerald ash borer, 60–61
Energy and the Environment
    (journal), 37
energy audits, in New York City, 78
Environmental Protection Agency,
    U.S., 82
Environment America, 76
extinctions, 57–58, 65
    caused by species' inability to
        adapt, 61–64

famine, after Medieval Warm Period,
    44–45
Fleischmann, Ken, 33
Ford, Henry, 14
Ford Motor Company, 14
forests, threats to, 59–60, 62
fossil fuels
    economic impacts of sudden
        cutback in, 46–47

global warming confirmed as
    consequence of burning of, 17
source of, 23
U.S. efforts to reduce emissions
    from, 67
worldwide consumption of, 46
fossil fuels industry
    attempts to discredit global
        warming by, 35–37
    lobbying for oil drilling in Arctic
        National Wildlife Refuge by, 72
Fourier, Jean Baptiste Joseph, 11
frogs, extinctions of, 58
fuel economy standards, effects on
    greenhouse gas emissions, 78

gasoline
    amount produced from barrel of
        oil, 47
    cost of, OPEC and, 50
Gelbspan, Ross, 37
Geological Survey, U.S., 72
Global Climate Change Impacts in the
    United States (U.S. Global Change
    Research Program), 43, 52
Global Climate Coalition, 35–37
global warming
    discovery of possibility of, 16–17
    environmental impacts of, 7–8
    governmental efforts to combat,
        66–68
    opinion on threat posed by, 27
global warming skeptics, 8–9, 18–19
    arguments of, 28–30, 46
    on errors in computer modeling,
        33–34
    views on species extinctions,
        61–64
Glover, Peter C., 8
Goodwin, Carte, 71
Gore, Al, 18, 28, 50, 51, 68
Government Accounting Office, U.S.
    (GAO), 9, 65
Gray, William, 46, 51
Great Barrier Reef, 53–55, **54**
greenhouse effect, 19, 22, 36
    first recognition of, 10–11

origin of phrase, 15
greenhouse gases, 7
   atmospheric, 15–17
   See also carbon dioxide
Gregory, Mike, 61
Gutro, Rob, 22

Hamilton, James D., 48–49
Hansen, James E., 10, 11, 18–19,
   23, 67
The Heat Is On (Gelbspan), 37
heat waves
   of 1988, 10
   of 2010, 20–21
Hendra virus, 59
Herms, Daniel, 60
hockey stick graph, 26–28, 38
   criticism of, 29, 31
Hughes, Lesley, 59
Hughes, Malcolm, 27, 28
humans, threats of displaced animals
   to, 59
Hurricane Ivan, 41
hydrofluorocarbons, 17

Industrial Age, 11–13
Inhofe, James, 38, 71, 72, 77
Institute for Energy Research, 80
Intergovernmental Panel on Climate
   Change (IPCC), 28, 30, 80
   revised predictions of, 33
internal combustion engine, 14
International Energy Agency (IEA),
   47, 50, 80
Introduction to Weather and Climate,
   An (Trewartha), 15
Inupiat people, 6–7, 9

jellyfish, 59
Jiang Gaoming, 42, 44
Jones, Phillip, 30–31, 38

Keeling, Charles, 15–16, 24, 34
Keeling Curve, 16, 17, 22
Kiehl, Jeffrey, 34
Kiyutelluk, Morris, 9
Kokeok, Shelton, 6–7
Kyoto Protocol (1997), 35–36, 68

Legates, David R., 28, 29
Little Ice Age (1600–1850), 28–29,
   32, 44–45, 65
Liu Shyh-fang, 66
Lohani, Shubash, 25
Lomborg, Bjørn, 19, 61, 64, 74
Lubchenco, Jane, 44

malaria, 59
Mann, Michael, 27, 28, 30, 31
Markey, Edward J., 71
Martell, Gail, 19
mean temperature change, 12
Medieval Warm Period (800–1400),
   28, 29, 44, 45, 65
methane, as percentage of all
   greenhouse gases, 17
Meyer, Warren, 33, 44, 45
Michaels, Patrick J., 30
Monbiot, George, 36–37
Monteverde Cloud Forest Preserve
   (Costa Rica), 58
mosquitoes, 59
Müller-Kraenner, Sascha, 73
Murkowski, Lisa, 73, 77

National Academy of Sciences, 17
National Aeronautics and Space
   Administration (NASA), 12, 81
natural gas, 47
Netherlands, threat of rising sea levels
   in, 40–41
nitrous oxide, as percentage of all
   greenhouse gases, 17
nuclear power, 47

Obama, Barack, 68–69
oil. *See* crude oil
oil well, first commercial, **13**
Olivier, Joseph, 75
On the Influence of Carbonic Acid in
   the Air upon the Temperature on the
   Ground (Arrhenius), 15, 16
opinion polls. *See* surveys
Organization of Petroleum Exporting
   Countries (OPEC), 50
   1973 oil embargo by, 48

Pennsylvania, effort to promote renewable energy in, 76
perfluorocarbons, 17
pine bark beetles, 59–60, 62
Plimer, Ian, 26, 55, 59
polar bears, 55–56, 64, 65
polls. *See* surveys
Pomerance, Rafe, 71
Pope, Carl, 69

Reay, David, 69
renewable energy, 18
    efficiency of, 70
    mandates for, 76, 78
        opposition to, 76
    percentage of U.S. energy provided by, 51
Ritzman, Dan, 72, 73
Rudd, Kevin, 74, 77

Sachs, Jeffrey, 49
Santer, Benjamin D., 36, 37
Sarichef Island (AK), 6–7, 9
    rate of coastal erosion on, 9
Schendler, Auden, 45
Schmidt, Gavin, 34, 55, 58
Scripps Institute of Oceanography, 20, 81
Shishmaref (AK), 6–7, **7**, 9
Singer, S. Fred, 11, 14, 18–19
skiing industry, 45, 52
Snetsinger, James, 62
solar energy, efficiency of, 70
Stop Global Warming, 81
sulfur hexafluoride, 17
surveys
    on impacts of global warming, 38
    on threat posed by global warming, 27

Taiwan, World Games Stadium in, 66, **67**, 78
Taylor, Mitchell, 56, 61
temperature(s)
    extreme, 10, 19, 20–21, 23
    mean change in, 12

Tibetan Plateau, 37
    glacial melting on, tracking of, 24–25, **25**
    impacts of glacial melting in, 38
Timofeeff, Peter, 39
Tishkov, Arkady, 19, 20
Trewartha, Glen Thomas, 15
Turkstra, Eelke, 41
Tyndall, James, 11, 34

United Nations Framework Convention on Climate Change, 81–82
United States
    carbon dioxide emissions by, 75
    efforts to reduce fossil fuel emissions by, 67
    renewable energy as percentage of total energy in, 51

Veron, Charlie, 56
Volstok station (Antarctica), 23

Waxman, Henry, 71
Weart, Spencer R., 17
weather
    catastrophic, costs of, 52
    climate versus, 21–22
    See also temperature(s)
Weller, Gunter, 8
West Virginia, resistance to renewable energy initiatives in, 77
Wilcox, Eric, 26
wind energy, efficiency of, 70
woolly mammoth, 62–64
World Conservation Union, 65
World Games Stadium (Kaohsiung, Taiwan), 78
World Health Organization (WHO), 59
World Meteorological Society, 23
World Wildlife Fund, 78
Wuebbles, Donald, 43

Yangtze River flooding, 42, **43**
Yao Tandong, 24

About the Author

A former newspaper reporter and columnist, Hal Marcovitz is the author of more than 150 books for young readers. He makes his home in Chalfont, Pennsylvania, with his wife Gail and daughter Ashley.